THE
BASSET HOUND

By MARCIA A. FOY
and ANNA KATHERINE NICHOLAS

Cover photo: *Left to right*, Mac Joy's Coke Is It, Ch. Jer Cal's Talk of the Town, and Diane's Funny Valentine, C.D., are three of the handsome Basset Hounds owned by Diane and Doug Fuerst, Mac-Joy Bassets, Ronkonkoma, N.Y.

Title page photo:
Am. and Can. Ch. Tal-E-Ho's Prancer, 7/16/70-2/26/80, one of the great dogs of this breed, was the sire of forty American Champions. Bred, owned and loved by Henry and Ann Jerman, West Islip, New York.

Back cover photo: Timber Ridge Basset Pack. Amelia F. Rogers, Hampstead, Maryland, Master and Huntsman.

ISBN 0-86622-044-5

© 1985 by T.F.H. Publications, Inc. Ltd.

Distributed in the UNITED STATES by T.F.H. Publications, Inc., 211 West Sylvania Avenue, Neptune City, NJ 07753; in CANADA by H & L Pet Supplies Inc., 27 Kingston Crescent, Kitchener, Ontario N2B 2T6; Rolf C. Hagen Ltd., 3225 Sartelon Street, Montreal 382 Quebec; in ENGLAND by T.F.H. Publications Limited, 4 Kier Park, Ascot, Berkshire SL5 7DS; in AUSTRALIA AND THE SOUTH PACIFIC by T.F.H. (Australia) Pty. Ltd., Box 149, Brookvale 2100 N.S.W., Australia; in NEW ZEALAND by Ross Haines & Son, Ltd., 18 Monmouth Street, Grey Lynn, Auckland 2 New Zealand; in SINGAPORE AND MALAYSIA by MPH Distributors (S) Pte., Ltd., 601 Sims Drive, # 03/07/21, Singapore 1438; in the PHILIPPINES by Bio-Research, 5 Lippay Street, San Lorenzo Village, Makati Rizal; in SOUTH AFRICA by Multipet Pty. Ltd., 30 Turners Avenue, Durban 4001. Published by T.F.H. Publications Inc. Manufactured in the United States of America by T.F.H. Publications, Inc.

Dedication

To all of the Bassets we've judged and admired in the show ring, to the breeders, and to the family Bassets who are adding such great pleasure to the lives of their owners.

In Appreciation

To all of you who have helped us assemble interesting material for this book, even though it may have been but a single photograph, we extend deep and sincere appreciation.

Very special thanks go (in alphabetical order) to Eric George, Kay Green, Meena Rogers, and Dr. and Mrs. Leonard Skolnick who have been tremendously cooperative in loaning us informative material about not only their own dogs but also various other dogs and aspects of the fancy. We are grateful to Jean Sheehy for lists and advice and to Peg Walton for all she has done to add valuable facts, photos, and information. The response to the announcement that such a book as this was forthcoming were truly heartwarming. We hope that all of you, and all our other readers, will feel that it is a worthwhile addition to literature dealing with this marvelous breed of hound.

Marcia Foy
Anna Katherine Nicholas

Contents

About the Authors

Marcia A. Foy

Marcia A. Foy was born in Chicago and raised in the suburbs of the North Shore. From early childhood she loved dogs and had many breeds at one time or another as pets, including Pekes, a Basset, a Gordon Setter, and Miniature Poodles.

Her first show dog was a Kerry Blue Terrier, That's Dundel of Delwin, who came from the noted Delwin Kennels of Ed Sayres, Sr. She showed this dog for the first time in 1945, when she was eleven years old.

Marcia moved East in 1960, at which time she acquired her first Beagles. Among those she has owned and shown are the unforgettable Champion Kings Creek Triple Threat; his son Champion Rockaplenty's Wild Oats (who now belongs to A.K.N.); the magnificent bitch, Trippe's daughter, Champion Foyscroft Triple Lena Wor Lo; the multi-Group winners Champion Junior's Foyscroft Wild Kid and the 13″ Champion Jo Mar's Repeat Performance: and many others. Although she has raised only a limited number of litters, she has bred a goodly number of champions, among them dogs who have provided foundation stock for other successful kennels.

Interest in Beagles is shared by a very special love of Poodles, a breed which has long been one of her favorites.

It was in 1976 that Marcia officiated for the first time as a judge, an experience which she has grown to thoroughly enjoy. Her first breeds were Beagles and Dachshunds. Currently she is approved for all Hounds and the Hound Group, the majority of the Terriers, and Best in Show. Her judging assignments take her on a wide course of travel each year, and she has officiated at leading shows throughout the United States and in most of Canada. One of her earliest assignments was that of the National Beagle Club Sweepstakes at Aldie, and she has also judged the Blossom Valley Beagle Club Specialty in California, along with dozens of all-breed shows.

Marcia has been largely instrumental in having persuaded the Southern New York Beagle Club, of which she is an Honorary Member, to hold an annual conformation Specialty, which it now does in conjunction with the Westchester Kennel Club each September— most successfully, we might add!

Anna Katherine Nicholas

Since early childhood, Anna Katherine Nocholas has been involved with dogs. Her first pets were a Boston Terrier, an Airedale, and a German Shepherd. Then, in 1925, came the first of the Pekingese—a gift from a friend who raised them. Now her home is shared with a Miniature Poodle and a dozen or so Beagles, including her noted Best in Show dog and National Specialty winner, Champion Rockaplenty's Wild Oats, a Gold Certificate sire (one of the breed's truly great stud dogs), who as a show dog was Top Beagle in the Nation in 1973. She also owns Champion Foyscroft True Blue Lou, Foyscroft Aces Are Wild, and in co-ownership with Marcia Foy, who lives with her, Champion Foyscroft Triple Mitey Migit.

Miss Nicholas is best known throughout the Dog Fancy as a writer and as a judge. Her first magazine article, published in *Dog News* magazine around 1930, was about Pekingese; and this was followed by a widely acclaimed breed column, "Peeking at the Pekingese" which appeared for at least two decades, originally in *Dogdom*, then, following the demise of that publication, in *Popular Dogs*. During the 1940's she was Boxer columnist for *Pure-Bred Dogs/American Kennel Gazette* and for *Boxer Briefs*. More recently many of her articles, geared to interest fanciers of every breed, have appeared in *Popular Dogs, Pure-Bred Dogs/American Kennel Gazette, Show Dogs, Dog Fancy*, and *The World of the Working Dog*. Currently she is a featured regular columnist in *Kennel Review, Dog World, Canine Chronicle* and *The Dog Fancier* (Canadian). Her *Dog World* column, "Here, There and Everywhere," was the Dog Writers Association of America winner of the Best Series in a Dog Magazine Award for 1979.

It was during the late 1930's that Miss Nicholas' first book, *The Pekingese*, appeared, published by and written at the request of the Judy Publishing Company. This book completely sold out and is now a collector's item, as is her *The Skye Terrier Book*, which was published by the Skye Terrier Club of America during the early 1960's.

In 1970 Miss Nicholas won the Dog Writers Association of America award for the Best Technical Book of the Year with her *Nicholas Guide to Dog Judging*, published by Howell Book House. In 1979 the revision of this book again won the Dog Writers Association of America Best Technical Book Award, the first time ever that a revision has been so honored by this association.

In the early 1970's, Miss Nicholas co-authored, with Joan Brearley, five breed books which were published by T.F.H. Publications, Inc. These were *This is the Bichon Frise, The Wonderful World of Beagles and Beagling* (winner of a Dog Writers Association of America Honorable Mention Award), *The Book of the Pekingese, The Book of the Boxer,* and *This is the Skye Terrier.*

During recent years, Miss Nicholas has been writing books consistently for T.F.H. These include *Successful Dog Show Exhibiting, The Book of the Rottweiler, The Book of the Poodle, the Book of the Labrador Retriever, The Book of the English Springer Spaniel, The Book of the Golden Retriever,* and *The Book of the German Shepherd Dog.* Most recently she has written *The Book of the Shetland Sheepdog,* another breed spectacular, and in the same series with the one you are now reading, *The Chow Chow, The Keeshond, The Cocker Spaniel,* and several additional titles. In the T.F.H. "KW" series, she has done *Rottweilers, Weimaraners* and *Norwegian Elkhounds.* She has also supplied the American chapters for two English publications imported by T.F.H., *The Staffordshire Bull Terrier* and *The Jack Russell Terrier.*

Miss Nicholas, in addition to her four Dog Writers Association of America awards, has on two occasions been honored with the *Kennel Review* "Winkie" as Dog Writer of the Year; and in both 1977 and 1982 she was recipient of the Gaines "Fido" award as Journalist of the Year in Dogs.

Her judging career began in 1934 at the First Company Governors' Foot Guard in Hartford, Connecticut, drawing the largest Pekingese entry ever assembled to date at this event. Presently she is approved to judge all Hounds, Terriers, Toys, and Non-Sporting Dogs; all Pointers, English and Gordon Setters, Vizslas, Weimaraners, and Wire-haired Pointing Griffons in Sporting breeds; and, in Working Group, Boxers and Doberman Pinschers. In 1970 she became the third woman in history to judge Best in Show at the prestigious Westminster Kennel Club Dog Show, where she has officiated on some sixteen other occasions through the years. In addition to her numerous Westminster assignments, Miss Nicholas has judged at such other outstandingly important events as Santa Barbara, Trenton, Chicago International, the Sportsmans in Canada, the Metropolitan in Canada, and Specialty Shows in several dozen breeds both in the United States and in Canada. She has judged in almost every one of the mainland United States and in four Canadian provinces, and her services are constantly sought in other countries.

Basset-Griffon Vendeen.

Basset d'Artois.

Chapter 1

The Origin of the Basset Hound

In a treatise on badger hunting, back in the general period of 1585, there was featured a woodcut depicting a sportsman in his "charette de chasse" with his badger dogs. The latter are said to have been clearly recognizable as Bassets, and it is widely believed that this was the first published drawing of the breed.

References to early Bassets are found in the writings of Arrian (around 125 A.D.), Oppian (some 25 years later), and Sir Thomas Cockaine (in 1591), all substantiating the antiquity of these dogs. Basset history has been delved into by several modern writers preceding us, and the stories make fascinating (if sometimes a bit contradictory) reading. We, however, do not intend to make this an in-depth study of these early times, as our space is limited and we feel that we prefer to concern ourselves primarily with the modern Basset as the breed is known by our readers today.

At least two types of Basset, a smooth variety and a rough-coated variety, were known in France by the mid-nineteenth century, enjoying popularity there. The smooth went under the collective heading of "Basset Francois." The rough was known as the "Basset Griffon." A further division also took place based on the formation of their forelegs. The shortest legged hound, with the most crooked forelegs, was a "Basset a Jambes Tordues." The longest legged dog, in whom this feature combined with the least bend of foreleg, was a "Basset a Jambes Droites." Between the two was a dog with moderately bent legs of medium length known as the "Basset a Jambes demi Tordues."

Wide variances in temperament and personality exist between the smooth Basset and the rough-coated Basset, we are told, almost to the point of their seeming like entirely different breeds. The smooth is every inch a typical hound, with all the characteristics of his kind. The rough, on the other hand, shares many characteristics with terriers, including a less calm disposition and a temperament more difficult for the huntsman to control. Thus the two hunt quite differently. The smooth Basset follows the traditional hound pattern, while the rough conducts himself more like a terrier in the field.

Bassets were so named by the French owing to their shortness of leg. "Bas" means "low" in French, an appropriate reference to the low-set build of these dogs. There are many variations of Basset said to have existed in France during pre-Revolutionary days, one count being as high as twelve. These dogs have obviously existed for a very long time. One popular theory was that they, and all other hounds of the type we now think of as "scent hounds," came directly from the St. Hubert Hound, owing to certain mutual characteristics and the fact that the St. Huberts have been proved to date back to the eighth century. Others are of different opinion. Speculation will probably continue indefinitely, for who is to say for certain exactly what sequence of events took place?

The French aristocracy of pre-Revolutionary days became great admirers of the sturdily built, low-slung massive little hounds which accompanied them so efficiently and amusingly on boar-hunting expeditions—just as did the English in their turn. Most sportsmen included at least several Bassets in their kennel for those occasions when they preferred setting out on foot rather than on horseback after hare, rabbits, and other small game.

History tells us that two very prominent Frenchmen, the Comte le Couteulx and M. Lane, played a major role in the development of the forebears of the modern English and American Basset. Both were prominent breeders with strong preferences as to the features they wished emphasized in their dogs, thus both were highly influential. The Couteulx-type hound was noted for the down-faced look and sad expression now considered so typically "Basset," with deep-set dark eyes, prominent haw, and a long deep head, narrow in width, so similar to the look of the Bloodhound. The Lane-type hound, on the other hand, had a quite different type head; it was wider in skull with a shorter ear and a larger, quite round eye. These dogs are said to have been usually of less striking color and also possessed an inclination toward knuckling over of the forelegs. Nonetheless, both types had their admirers!

12

Chapter 2

The Basset's Development in Great Britain

Early History

The first Bassets recorded as having been imported into England fron France were a couple who became known in history as Basset and Belle. These were acquired by Lord Galway as a gift from the pack of the Marquis de Tournon and the Comte de Tournon, the result of a promise made during a visit by Lord Galway to France several months prior to the arrival of the dogs at his kennel.

From this couple Lord Galway produced a litter of five, which was sold in its entirety to Lord Onslow, who added several more from the Tournon pack and from the hounds of the Comte de Couteulx, forming a splendid pack of his own on French bloodlines which he used for hare hunting until 1882 when he dispersed the pack after he had been offered and accepted a Harrier mastership.

Everett Millais, already aware of and interested in Bassets, acquired some of Lord Onslow's pack at this time, as did Mr. Krehl, who is credited with having been behind the formation of the Basset Hound Club.

Royal approval was accorded the talents of the breed when the Prince and Princess of Wales founded a small pack. And Queen Alexandra appreciated and raised them at the royal kennel.

We have seen Sir Everett Millais referred to frequently as the "father of the breed" in Great Britain; and after studying the facts in

13

earlier Basset writings, we fully understand why. A widely quoted letter from Sir Everett written during 1894 to Mr. Croxton-Smith reveals much of interest regarding Basset activities during that period and the years immediately preceding it. In the letter, Sir Everett refers to his first Basset, obtained twenty years earlier, when the hound attracted his attention while being exhibited in the kennel department of the Jardin d'Acclimatation. This was the famous dog named Model, and he won his owner over completely from his previous interest in

Two typical Walhampton Bassets who were exported to America by Lt. Col. Christopher Heseltine.

Dachshunds. Although there had been some Bassets in England prior to Model's arrival, he was the first to be shown, in 1875, where he attracted a goodly amount of attention and was widely admired. Model had come from the kennel of the Comte de Couteulx. A problem arose for Sir Everett however with Model's arrival. Sir Everett was, naturally, anxious to breed only purebred Bassets, and upon inquiry he discovered that Model was actually the only one to be found in Great Britain at that particular time. Serious discussion of what course to follow took place between Sir Everett and knowledgeable dog men of the day. A sportsman for whom he held particular respect, Mr. Lort, gave him the advice he finally followed, which was that it would not be unsuitable to breed a Basset to a large Beagle. Sir Everett did so, with the result that at the 1877 Agricultural Hall, he was able to show second-generation hounds so close to Basset type that it is said to have been impossible to recognize the fact that the outcross had been introduced. However, with the acquisition by Lord Onslow of the true French-bred hounds, straight from the kennel which had produced Model (that of the Comte de Couteulx), Sir Everett abandoned breeding the strain with which he had been working, concentrating then on pure Basset lines. These dogs of Lord Onslow's were named Fino and Finette. The latter was duly bred to Model, with the result that Sir Everett acquire his first purebred Basset bitch, Garenne; and from the same litter Lord Onslow kept Proctor.

Garenne was bred back to her sire, Model, and in 1878 produced Isabel, who the following year became the dam of several puppies sired by Fino. These, added to those already part of his pack, enabled Sir Everett to guarantee the first Basset class in England, at Wolverhampton in 1880.

During this same period, Lord Onslow had also been breeding to an imported hound called Juno who was a prolific producer. This bitch, bred to Proctor, brought forth Cigarette, whose principal claim to fame would seem to have come by way of her daughter, Medore.

1880 was a year during which several Bassets were imported into Great Britain. Among these were Fino de Paris (as I understand it, a different dog from the original Fino referred to above—"Fino" was a much used name in early Basset breeding) who Sir Everett understood to have been his Model's brother. Along with him came Guinevere, his great-granddaughter. These two eventually produced Champion Bourbon and Fino V. The aforementioned Cigarette was bred to Bourbon, which brought about the famous Medore, in her turn bred to

Ch. Walhampton Linguist, a member of the famed pack owned by Major Godfrey Heseltine.

Fino VI (son of Fino V ex Vivian, a Fino de Paris granddaughter). It was from this latter litter that Champions Forester, Fresco, Merlin, and Flora resulted.

Champion Forester's influence on Bassets was inestimable. Through his sons and daughters, nearly every important Basset of the late 1800's descended from him and thus traced back to Champion Fino de Paris, Model, and to Lord Onslow's early hounds.

Sir Everett, as he states in his letter, "had a share in the breeding of Proctor," but he salutes Lord Onslow as the breeder of Cigarette, Mr. Herbert Watson as the breeder of Medore, Mr. Krehl as the breeder of Fino V and Fino VI, and Mr. F.B. Craven for the litter which included Forester.

The very first Basset hunt to be registered in *Bailey's Directory* was founded in 1889 by Tom and Mornington Cannon. Probably one of the most famed and admired Basset packs of all time (and certainly the finest of its day) was Walhampton, founded on nine and a half couples purchased from the Cannons plus a couple which had been a gift from Captain Peacock, M.F.H., to the brothers Lt. Colonel Christopher and Major Godfrey Heseltine. From 1890 until the death of Major Godfrey Heseltine in 1932, this pack was hunted regularly (except during the time of World War I), and they were outstanding for the quality of their work and for their handsome looks, having been bred with both in mind.

Lt. Col. Christopher Heseltine was the huntsman, and his brother the M.B.H. Major Godfrey Heseltine was famous around the world for his thorough knowledge of hare hunting, which was his principal and tremendously enjoyed hobby.

The Walhampton Bassets won Challenge Prizes as Champion Dog Hound and Champion Bitch Hound, along with honors for their puppies, and for Best Couple Hounds at Masters of Basset Hounds Association Hound Shows at Banbury. Additionally, in the eleven years between 1921 and Major Heseltine's death in 1932, they won no less than 27 Challenge Certificates on the British show bench. Walhampton was the only one of the early Basset packs to have survived for a considerable length of time. It is interesting to note that around 1900 Christopher Heseltine took on another hound pack, with the result that when Major Godfrey Heseltine was sent to a post in India during 1903, he sold his Bassets to Marquis Conyngham, who continued to hunt them. This was only temporary, for when Major Heseltine returned home in 1910 the first thing he did was to re-purchase his Bassets and reestablish them.

The Walhamptons even played their part in World War I, having been loaned to the Royal Navy! Those of us who are Cecil Alden fans will be interested to learn that during two seasons he spent in India following the war years, Major Heseltine left the Walhamptons with his friend Cecil and that Cecil evidently greatly enjoyed the experience.

Following Major Heseltine's death, the pack was sold and the hounds quite widely dispersed. A few, however, remained in England; they were purchased by Colonel Marrison, who later took in as partners Mrs. Groom and then Lt. Colonel Breirmeyer, by whom they were carried on. The Walhampton prefix was dropped and the new name became Westerby in honor of the town through which the hounds frequently traveled.

The rough Basset (Basset Griffon) enjoyed popularity in England toward the close of the nineteenth century, but following World War I it was seldom seen there. Some of the first roughs exhibited in England were owned by the Reverend J.C. Macdona and by Dr. Seton. One named Romano, and registered in the Kennel Club Stud Book, has been described as an especially nice one.

In 1892, a collection of the rough-coated Bassets was brought from France for exhibition at the Crufts Dog Show. A number of these were purchased, although we understand that the prices brought were probably disappointing to the sellers.

Queen Alexandra was an admirer of the Rough Basset and owned some splendid ones. Mr. Krehl had some good ones, too. Other owners included Mr. F. Lowe, Major H. Jones, Mr. C.C. Lawrence, and the Reverend W. Shield.

I believe that the first rough champions were Champion Tambour and Champion Pervenche, sire and dam of Champion Puritan. The latter, bred by Mrs. Tottie, was born in February 1897 and had completed championship prior to reaching one year's age. We have read that this dog was heavily boned, sound, of splendid quality, with a really good coat and rich tri-coloring.

What follows are descriptions of some successful British Basset Hounds. The breed would seem to be prospering nicely, and we have admired a number of the dogs from these kennels whose pictures are included for our readers to share and enjoy.

Brackenacre

Mr. and Mrs. J.F.C. (Jim and Marianne) Nixon are owners of some highly distinguished and very beautiful Basset Hounds at their Brackenacre Kennels in St. Budeaux, Plymouth, Devon.

The true foundation of the Bassets at this kennel is Champion Brackenacre Annabella, daughter of Hardacre Sungarth Eager from Brackenacre Kierhill Oonagh, who is to be found in the pedigree of every Brackenacre Basset.

Among the notable winners here, Champion Brackenacre The Viking holds pride of place. Co-owned by the Nixons and Mrs. M. Bews, this marvelous dog has won two dozen Challenge Certificates and eighteen Reserves, Best in Show at three breed championship events, Reserve Best in Show at Southern Counties all-breed championship

Brackenacre Sweet Pea (Ch. Brackenacre James Bond ex Brackenacre Kind of Bell) is a red and white multiple Best in Show winning bitch who has one C.C. and two Reserves to her credit as of May 1984. Owned by Mr. and Mrs. J.F.C. Nixon, Brackenacre Bassets, Plymouth, Devon, England. Photo by Diane Pearce.

Eng. Ch. Brackenacre Jessica (Ch. Brackenacre Fino de Paris ex Ch. Brackenacre Daisy Belle) with her champion Mini-Wire Dachshund friend, Miss Alliance. From the famed British kennel "Brackenacre" owned by Mr. and Mrs. J.F.C. Nixon at Plymouth, Devon. Photo by Diane Pearce.

Eng. Ch. Brackenacre James Bond (Ch. Brackenacre Fino de Paris ex Brackenacre Emma Peel) is a Best in Show, Best of Breed and multiple Hound Group winner along with being the sire of several champions. Owned by Mr. and Mrs. J.F.C. Nixon, Brackenacre Bassets, Plymouth, Devon, England. Photo by Diane Pearce.

show, multiple Bests in Show at open events, and Best of Breed at Crufts in 1984. He is a son of Champion Brackenacre James Bond (by Champion Brackenacre Fino de Paris from Brackenacre Emma Peel, who is himself a Best in Show winner), and his dam is Witchacre Magpie of Brackenacre.

Other Best in Show winners owned by the Nixons include Champion Brackenacre Jessica, Brackenacre Sweet Pea, Champion Brackenacre Primrose, and Champion Brackenacre James Bond.

In 1982 the Nixons won the following Basset Hound Club annual awards: Basset of the Year (Viking), Brood Bitch of the Year (Magpie), Stallion Hound of the Year (James Bond), and Breeders of the Year.

Orakei

Miss Frances Muirhead, Orakei, Cromer, Norfolk, is one of England's highly enthusiastic Basset owners. Her principal dog is Brewerscote The Norfeman of Orakei, who represents some of the best known and most highly successful British Basset bloodlines.

"Bertie" is a Best of Breed winner and has placed in all of the shows he has attended. Most of his awards were won in Variety Classes, up against other hound breeds. Miss Muirhead remarks that not many Bassets have been shown in Variety Classes in England, but it is necessary that "Bertie" do so at the shows near home as no classes for Bassets are provided within a hundred miles of where Miss Muirhead's kennels are located.

Puppies by this superbly bred dog are looked forward to with keen anticipation. His sire is Champion Brackenacre The Viking, by Champion Brackenacre James Bond. His dam, Champion Bezel Isabella, goes back to Brackenacre, Ireton, and Fredwell bloodlines.

The only SHOW Basset in the county of Norfolk in England, Brewerscote The Norfeman of Orakei is owned by Orakei Kennels, Miss Frances Muirhead, at Cromer.

Siouxline Matthew, English Challenge Certificate winner with numerous honors to his credit, bred and owned by Mrs. Sue Ergis, Poole, Dorset, England.

Siouxline

Siouxline Bassets are located at Poole, Dorset, England, where they are owned by Sue Ergis.

Two very handsome homebreds are currently in the limelight for this kennel as we go to press—Siouxline Matthew and The Senator of Siouxline. Interestingly, both of these dogs have as their great grand-sires American Champion Lyn-Mar Acres Endman and American Champion Long View Acres Bonza.

Siouxline Matthew is by English Champion Langpool Scrumpy ex Siouxline Kelly. He was born in December 1979; and his wins include

The Senator of Siouxline, a very exciting young English Basset, bred and owned by Mrs. Sue Ergis, Poole, Dorset, England.

one Challenge Certificate, one Reserve Challenge Certificate, one Best in Show (an all-breed open show), four Reserve Bests in Show (all-breed open shows), fifteen Bests of Breed, and a Junior Warrant (when ten months of age).

The Senator of Siouxline, by Verwood Varne ex Siouxline Miriam, was born in April 1982. He gained a Challenge Certificate when six and a half months of age at the Midland Basset Hound Club Championship Show, where he also went on to Best in Show and Best Puppy in Show. He also has a Reserve Challenge Certificate and a Junior Warrant (gained at nine months), and he won first in the Puppy Class at Crufts in 1983 and first in the Yearling Class there in 1984—a young dog to watch for in the future!

Tancegem

Mrs. Tanya Polkinghorne owns the Tancegem Bassets at Truro, Cornwall, England, which is headed by the lovely Best in Show bitch Champion Brackenacre Primrose, co-owned by her breeders, Mr. and Mrs. Nixon.

Primrose won her first Challenge Certificate at the Leicester Championship Show in 1980 under judge Evan Roberts; her second at Paignton in 1981 under judge Margaret Thorley; and her third, to complete title, at Belfast in 1983 under judge Marion Spavin. She is also a Best in Show winner at all-breed open shows.

It is not only as a show bitch, however, that Primrose has been successful! She was bred to multiple Best in Show winning and Top Winning 1983 Basset in England, Champion Brackenacre The Viking, an interesting line-breeding as Viking's dam and Primrose's sire are littermates. The results have been very pleasing, as they produced the striking young bitch Tancegem's Morvoren, who at her first championship show in 1984, the Basset Hound Club Specialty, was Best Junior

Tancegem's Morvoren, bred and owned by Tanya Polkinghorne, at the Basset Hound Club 30th Anniversary Championship Show in 1984, here taking **Best Junior Bitch, Best Debutante Bitch and Best Special Breeders Bitch.**

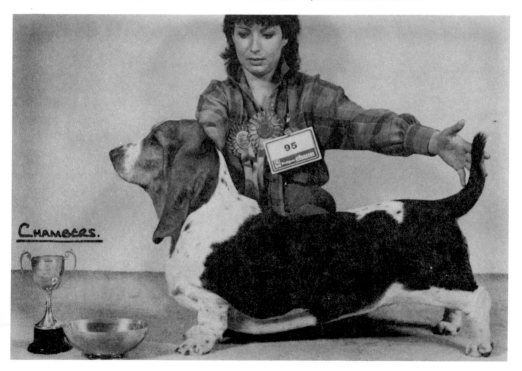

Eng. Ch. Brackenacre Primrose with co-owner Mrs. T. Polkinghorne. Primrose is co-owned with her breeders, Mr. and Mrs. Nixon.

Bitch, Best Debutante Bitch, and Best Breeders Bitch. Mrs. Polkinghorne points out that this is another classic example that one need not be involved in a breed for years before succeeding in producing a winner, as Morvoren was in the very first litter of Bassets she has bred. Just at the start of her career she shows every promise of success, and a spectacular winning future is predicted for her.

Tancegem raises Mini Wire Dachshunds, too, and is currently Cornwall's top winning kennel in this breed as well as in Bassets.

Chapter 3

The Basset's Development in the United States

Early History

It was in 1885 that the first Basset Hounds were registered with the American Kennel Club. Bouncer, who received number 323, was a tricolor dog by Major from Venus, born March 1881. He was bred by Pottinger Dorsey of Newmarket, Maryland, and was owned by Colin Cameron of Brickville, Pennsylvania. Countess, a bitch by Nero from Lotta, was born in April 1880 and received 3235 as her assigned number. Her color was not listed. She was bred by E.S. Krecht in Germany and owned in the United States by B.F. Seitner of Dayton, Ohio.

It was obvious that Bassets had reached the United States earlier than 1885, however. George Washington is said to have received a number of them following the American Revolution, from his friend Lafayette in France. This is not surprising when one considers that General Washington's enjoyment of hounds was, and is, well known.

It has also been recorded that Lord Aylesford had an imported couple in 1883 at his Texas ranch with whom he hunted hare, and in that same year Champion Nemours was purchased from the well-known breeder George Krehl in England by Mr. Chamberlain who brought him to the Maizeland Kennels of Lawrence Timson in New Jersey.

Nemours was born in March 1883. All three of these were sired by Jupiter. A bitch named Vivien was the dam of Nemours.

A class for Bassets was offered at Westminster's 1884 event, where Champion Nemours was first seen by fanciers here. This dog was shown at Philadelphia and the National Breeders' Show, won at New Haven and Boston in 1885, and became a champion at Boston in 1886.

Among early importations was Bertrand, a son of Bourbon, and Canace, a daughter of Jupiter, during 1885. They went to a gentleman from New Haven, Connecticut, Mr. C.B. Gilbert. With them he produced Jose and Juan.

Ch. Seifenjagenheim Lazy Bones, by Ch. Lyn-Mar's Clown ex Ch. Webb's Black Amanda. Bred by Mr. and Mrs. John Seifen. Owned by Mr. Chris Teeter. Handled by Frank Hardy to a very impressive show career during the late 1950's. Photo from the collection of the late Frank and Dorothy Hardy.

Born Jan. 22nd 1940, Upland Lucky, bred by A.W. Porter, by Stockford Duke (Ch. Reddy II ex Ch. Rebecca) from Stockford Lady (Walhampton Abbot—Music of Woodleigh), also combines Gerald Livingston's Kilsyth breeding in her pedigree. Photo courtesy of Meena Rogers.

It is interesting that in 1889 Mr. Charles Porter of Philadelphia showed at Westminster a dog named Merlin and a bitch named Babbette. Upland soon thereafter was adopted as Mr. Porter's kennel prefix; and at the Westminster Kennel Club Dog Show in 1943, almost the entire Basset entry, ten of them to be exact, were from Mr. and Mrs. Andrew W. Porter, Upland Farms, Chester, Pennsylvania, all of them carrying the Upland prefix and the majority homebred. Included among them were several by Champion Pennsy Boy ex Upland Lady and some by Stockdale Duke or from Stockford bitches. We assume Charles and Andrew W. Porter were father and son.

The other exhibitor at the 1943 Westminster was Mrs. Harold Fogleson of East Lansing, Michigan, her two entries a class bitch named Duchess of Greenly Hall, by Champion Duke of Greenly Hall ex Kiernan's Mitz; and a Specials dog, Champion Promise of Greenly Hall, by Nottke's Pat ex Champion Peg O'My Heart. Lee S. Wade was the handler.

An early important and influential Basset kennel was Kilsyth, owned by Gerald M. Livingston on Long Island and in Georgia. Many of us are more in the habit of thinking of the Livingstons in connection with other breeds—Mr. Livingston with Labrador Retrievers and Mrs. Livingston with various Toys—but Mr. Livingston was a keen enthusiast for Bassets, and he owned them over a number of years dating from his first importation in 1921. A catalogue of the 1937 Westminster reveals that Kilsyth Kennels were the only Bassets exhibited: two dogs and two bitches individually double entered in American-bred and Open Classes. All were homebred. The bitches, littermates, were Kilsyth Frills and Kilsyth Freckles, by Prince of Kilsyth ex Fanny, born February 26th 1933. The dogs were Kilsyth Broker (Kilsyth Bunker ex Kilsyth Fury) born in August 1931 and Kilsyth Senator (Kilsyth Bob ex Kilsyth Beauty II) born in September 1935. Mr. Livingston's foundation stock came principally from

Ch. Huey of Cypress, a Mon Philippe of Greenly Hall son, who with the lovely bitch Hamlin's Missie (daughter of Lyn Mar Acres Proximity) produced numerous important Basset champions of the 1950's-60's period. Among them Ch. Gwendolyn of Mandeville, and several others of note. Owned by Helen Nelson. Photo courtesy of Dr. and Mrs. Leonard Skolnick.

Walhampton, and among others he imported from there during the 1920's were English and American Champion Walhampton Andrew, Walhampton Dainty, and Walhampton Aaron; in addition, he also brought over the French Baillet's Brano.

Erastus Tefft imported heavily during the 1920's, too, including Champion Lavenham Pippin, said to have been undefeated either in England or in the United States. It is rumored that Mr. Tefft paid three thousand dollars for Pippin, quite a considerable sum in those pre-inflation days! He also bought Pippin's niece Walhampton Passion and, at the same time, Dalby Hall Drifter.

During this period a Mr. Smith also imported an imposing collection of Bassets from both England and France. And Walhampton Lively came from England to start Loren Free's kennel, Shellbark, in Ohio.

Mr. and Mrs. George Sloane, owners of Brookmead Kennels, which were also widely known for outstanding Schnauzers, took pride in their pack of Bassets which included Walhampton Linguist, sire of many of the great early importations and considered by authorities to be the best-headed Basset of his day. The excellent bitch Walhampton Alice was brought over for breeding, as was Walhampton Muffles who produced some good ones sired by Paris. The Sloanes' kennel was managed by Frank Brumby, younger brother to Leonard Brumby, Sr., and uncle to retired American Kennel Club Vice-President Leonard Brumby, Jr.

The Basset Hound Club of America was formed in the mid-1930's in Detroit, Michigan. Charter members were Mr. and Mrs. Alfred Bissell, B.F. Chaney, Harold R. Frazee, William Fritz, George C. Gregg, Carmon Klink, Alfred E. Kannowski. W.P. Klapp, Jr., James E. Lee, Ann Levy, Gerald M. Livingston, Carl Nottke, Effie Seitz, and Lewis Thompson. The first President was Mr. Fritz, Emil Seitz was the first Vice-President, and Carl Nottke was the first Treasurer. The Basset Hound Club of America is the parent club for the breed (thus responsible for the standard and any changes or revisions to it which may seem necessary). It holds field trials and conformation Specialty shows.

Regional clubs have gradually been recognized in many areas of the United States. These clubs conduct Specialty shows and, like the parent club, are dedicated to serving the best interest of the breed. Basset owners should find membership in any of these clubs helpful and beneficial.

Ch. The Ring's Ali Baba winning Best in Show at Old Dominion Kennel Club, April 1961. Jerry Rigden handling for Mrs. Frances Scaife.

The 1940's–1960's

We have already mentioned Mr. and Mrs. Andrew W. Porter and Mrs. Harold Fogleson as exhibitors at the 1943 Westminster. The following year, only one Basset was entered there, Mrs. Fogleson's Champion Promise of Greenly Hall (Nottke's Pat ex Champion Peg O'My Heart), a homebred born in May 1940.

Twenty-one Bassets turned out for the 1947 Westminster event at Madison Square Garden. Again Champion Promise of Greenly Hall was entered as a Special. Also the Belbay Bassets, from New Alexandria, Pennsylvania, were very much in evidence. Champion Brag-gelonne of Belbay, born in June 1933, was entered for Specials by Howard R. Morrison; and Champion Envy of Belbay, Champion Butz's Yankee Boy, and Champion Kelly's Kanjur were among the nine Bassets entered by Belbay Kennels. Mrs. M. Lynwood Walton was on the exhibitor's list that year with Soubrette of Lyn Mar and Chanson of Lyn Mar, littermates by Champion Promise of Greenly Hall. Ira D. Shoop, of Norristown, Pennsylvania, had Hartshead Pep-per (Fallowfield Reaper ex Hillcrest Gigolette) and Hartshead Ginger (Champion Hillcrest Charley Boy ex Hartshead Firefly), both bred by Emil Seitz.

There was also an entry from Mr. and Mrs. Bernal Thompson, Dunkirk, New York; and Mrs. Charles D. Plumb (more usually associated with Greyhounds) had Gravity.

In 1952, the nine Westminster Bassets included one of the eventual immortals of the breed, Champion Lyn Mar's Clown, owned by Mrs. M.L. Walton and sired by Gerald Livingston's Kilsyth Lucky from Champion Maitri of Lyn Mar. Other entries by Mrs. Walton were Duchess and Gossip, both of Lyn Mar Acres. Prankster of Lyn Mar Acres represented George O. Walbridge, II. Preux Chevalier of Lyn Mar Acres was entered by Morgan Hebard; and Mr. and Mrs. Hans Sonnental had Lyn Mar Acres Bazaar.

Others showing Bassets that same year were Frank Hardy and Kay Scallon, co-owners of Belbay Welcome; Dr. Pierre Morand, D.V.M., with Beaver Brook Merry Madcap; and Mrs. Lester Noel Webb, with Bose's Princess Patty.

In 1954, Mrs. Walton was back with Champion Gossip of Lyn Mar Acres (by Clown ex Duchess); and Edward M. Williamson had Cham-pion Wakem's Clarabelle, also by Champion Lyn Mar Clown, the dam in this case Champion Wakem's Sandra of Lyn Mar Acres.

A whole flock of names important to Basset history turned up in the 1956 Westminster catalogue! Among them was Chris Teeter with those two greats, Champion Seifenjagenheim Lazy Bones and Cham-pion Slowpoke Hubertus. Lazy Bones was by Champion Lyn Mar's Clown ex Champion Webb's Black Amanda (daughter of the bitch Mrs. Webb had Specialed at Westminster in 1952, Bose's Princess Patty). Slowpoke Hubertus was by Champion Hartshead Pepper ex Abigail of Woodleigh. Frank Hardy was instrumental in Mr. Teeter's purchase of these two dogs, and by the mid-1960's Mr. Teeter had made the imposing number of 51 champions. Lazy Bones sired 50 or

Since 1952, *Tropical Fish Hobbyist* has been the source of accurate, up-to-the-minute, and fascinating information on every facet of the aquarium hobby. Join the more than 50,000 devoted readers worldwide who wouldn't miss a single issue.

One of the most important Bassets in breed history, Ch. Abbot Run Valley Brassy, owned by Mr. and Mrs. Walter Brandt of Cumberland, R.I. He finished at 11 months of age with 5 majors, and became an impressive winner in Hound Group and Specialty Show. He produced 48 American champions. Brassy was a son of Ch. Lyn-Mar Acres Top Brass.

Ch. Look's Choice, by Ch. Andre of Greenly Hall ex Ch. Belbay Winning Look, was bred by Jean Sanger Look and owned by Dr. and Mrs. Vincent A. Nardiello, Jr. Handled here by Frank Hardy. From the collection of the late Dorothy and Frank Hardy.

more champions and became Top Basset during his campaigning days.

Then the Millvan Kennels, owned by Dr. and Mrs. Vincent A. Nardiello, Jr., of Glen Head, New York, were very much in evidence at this Westminster event and on the Eastern show scene generally over a number of years. Champion Look's Choice, by Champion Andre of Greenly Hill ex Champion Belbay Winning Look, gained about 100 Best of Breed awards and was as well a notable sire. Champion Millvan's Deacon, also owned by the Nardiellos, was a Best in Show winner; many other excellent Bassets were to be found at this noteworthy kennel. The Millvan dogs were handled by Walter C. Foster.

The owner of the sire of Champion Look's Choice, Jean S. Look, was located in the Carolinas and is another breeder whose impact on Bassets was both strong and favorable. Based on Belbay and Greenly Hall, her kennels were well known for achievements in both conformation and the field.

Mr. and Mrs. Franklin Heckler, of Chalfont, Pennsylvania, were breeders of importance, and Elva Heckler continued with the Elvalins on her own after Mr. Heckler died. Champion Look's Pensive of Elvalin and Champion Ploddalong of Elvalin were among her 1965 Westminster entries. It was a bitch from Elvalin, Champion Miss Linda Lovely, whom Bob Noerr bred to Champion Longview Acres Smokey to produce the history-making and unforgettable Champion The Ring's Ali Baba whom Jerry Rigden piloted to so exciting a show record for Mrs. Frances Scaife.

The Noerrs were Basset and Bloodhound enthusiasts, highly successful in both breeds. Mary Lees and Bob were very knowledgeable and talented fanciers. In addition to the Bassets already discussed, Champion The Ring's Banshee was another of particular note from this kennel. "Pride of place" must go, however, to Ali Baba, whose achievements in the dog show world were a credit to his breed.

Ali Baba was born in June 1957 and was acquired as a young dog by Mrs. Frances Scaife who placed him in Jerry Rigden's hands for his show career. Ali Baba amassed a total of more than 100 hound Groups during his lifetime, 49 of which were during 1962, earning him the Quaker Oats Award for the Eastern Division that year. He was also a multiple all-breed and Specialty Best in Show winner, and he was the winner of the first Potomac Basset Hound Club Specialty.

Abbot Run Valley Kennels made a very important position for themselves in the Basset world, as one will note in reading our kennel histories. Walter and Marjorie Brandt were talented breeders, keenly interested in hunting with their dogs and the first to appreciate the Basset's potential as an obedience dog. They helped at least several other exceptionally fine breeders off to a good start, and they themselves became popular, knowledgeable judges.

Lime Tree, owned by Mr. and Mrs. Robert V. Lindsay of Syosset, New York, was another important kennel of this period. Mrs. Lindsay achieved considerable success with her dogs (she, too, combined an enthusiasm for both Bassets and Bloodhounds) and was successful at the shows with her Champion Lime Tree Micawber, by Champion Seifenjagenheim Lazy Bones from Champion Lyn Mar Acres Zephyr.

Kay Ellenberger had one of the nicest Bassets of that period on the East Coast in her Long Island kennel; this Basset, Champion Talleyrand Keene was a consistent winner for her.

Helen and Clip Boutell were breeders whom the authors recall with admiration for their talents and dedication. Double B Kennels, as theirs was known, had an especially attractive homebred champion in their Double B's Ishmael. The kennel was very active until Helen Boutell's untimely death, and although not active since then as breeders, Clip Boutell, (who passed away only recently), and their daughter Chrissy shared very enthusiastically in the hobby.

Joseph and Mercedes Braun came into Bassets sometime during this period, and they have certainly been assets to the breed. Mrs. Braun is the author of another splendid book on Bassets and both she and her husband are sought-after and knowledgeable judges.

James Lindley II (not to be confused with the Lindsays) had fine dogs and was devoted to the breed. We especially recall his Champion Lindley's Lucky Lindy Lou. Mrs. Oley Benson had Hound Hollow Bassets, including the imported Champion Rossingham Blessing, his son, and his grandson.

Santana-Mandeville, owned by Mr. and Mrs. Paul Nelson, definitely deserves credit for the quality of its especially beautiful and dominant Bassets which first appeared under the joint kennel name in the late 1950's. Champion Santana-Mandeville's Sweet Pea (bred by Mr. and Mrs. John A. Brady, by the great Champion Santana's Count Dracula from Mandeville's Pretty Penelope) and Champion Santana-Mandeville Mark (by Dracula from the fabulous bitch Champion Gwendolyn of Mandeville) were two they had entered in Westminster 1959. You will read more of the Santana-Mandeville dogs in the Skolnick's Slippery Hill kennel story.

Ch. Bar-Wick's Reba Ridge, by Ch. Tal-E-Ho's Charger ex Ch. Bar-Wick's Miss Met, was born in 1973, bred by Barbara Wicklund and Marjorie M. Brandt, owned by Barbara and Alfred A. Wicklund, Neshanic Station, New Jersey. Handled by Patricia Laurans.

Chapter 4

Some Well-Known Kennels in the United States

It is the authors' feeling that one of the best of all ways to describe the progress of a breed is by telling our readers of the individual breeders and kennels that have contributed well to its progress along the way. Thus we are proud to present many important Bassets and summaries of the backgrounds from which their successes have been attained. Not all of the kennels are still active, but each has contributed to the well-being and development of these splendid dogs. Study these pages well and you will come away with an increased knowledge of where the best Basset Hounds have been bred, the care and forethought expended towards their progress and improvement generation after generation, and the exciting results of the efforts of these breeders.

Along with the brief descriptions of long-time breeders, we also pay tribute to the comparative newcomers. On their shoulders squarely rests the task of carrying on and preserving what has already been accomplished and the responsibility for the future well-being of the breed.

Bar-Wick

The Bar-Wick Bassets, at Neshanic Station, New Jersey, belong to Barbara Wicklund, who has been active in the breed since the late 1960's.

Ch. Bar-Wick's Miss Met, by Ch. Ebenezer of Hampden Meadows ex Ch. Bar-Wick's Hey Sandy, was whelped in 1969, bred by Alfred A. Wicklund and Marjorie M. Brandt, owned by Barbara Wicklund and M.M. Brandt.

Champion Abbot Run Valley Pamela was Barbara's foundation bitch. She was bred to Champion Abbot Run Valley Brassy, producing Champion Bar-Wick's Hey Sandy. In her turn, Sandy bred to Champion Hampden Meadows Ebenezer (a Brassy grandson) produced the lovely Champion Bar-Wick's Miss Met.

Miss Met bred to Champion Tal-E-Ho's Charger produced Champion Bar-Wick's Reba Ridge, whom Mrs. Wicklund considers to be her "best ever," and Champion Bar-Wick's First Baseman.

First Baseman completed championship at thirteen months of age with four majors including two Specialties. He was campaigned sparingly but came out again for the National Specialty in 1980 and 1981, winning first in the Veterans Class on both occasions.

From the only two litters he sired, Baseman produced four champions to date with others on the way. A grandson of his, who recently finished at one year of age, has Group placements to his credit at fourteen months, while a granddaughter was Winners Bitch and Best of Opposite Sex at the Potomac Basset Hound Club Specialty in April 1984.

Champion Wagtail's Rise and Shine, sired by First Baseman now being shown with notable success, is the current star at Bar-Wick.

Beartooth

Beartooth Basset Kennels, owned and operated by Dr. Byron and Carole Sue Wisner, are located seven miles from Billings, Montana, near the beautiful Beartooth Mountains.

The Wisners "discovered" Bassets while Dr. Wisner was a resident in oral surgery at Ohio State University. Another resident owned one with which Byron was promptly fascinated, thus beginning a series of

Ch. Beartooth Pia is one of the Wisners' favorite bitches. Ch. Beartooth Victor is her sire—Oranpark Gloria her dam.

Ch. Beartooth Ulrick, by Ch. Beartooth Raymond, is the newest Beartooth Group winner. He is out of Beartooth Elaine owned by the Wisners and Dave and Patty Crumrine, Parvell, Wyoming.

Sunday afternoon visits to the Margem Hills Kennels of Marg Patterson at Columbus. With each visit his enthusiasm for the breed seemed to grow. A male pup by International and American Champion Sir Tomo of Glenhaven was reserved for him and a bitch by Champion Willstone Harvey came next.

When Byron had completed his residency, he and Carole packed up their three-month-old puppy, Sir Zachary of Margem Hills, three cats (one of which delivered seven kittens on the day after their arrival in Billings), and a Volkswagon full of Byron's tropical fish (in cartons) and headed west. When the pack grew to eight—Zachary, two bitches from Margem Hills (one of them the bitch who was to become Beartooth's foundation, Margem Hills Hustlin Harriat, ROM), two champions from Nancy Evans Kennels, a Slippery Hill bitch, and two pups from a litter sired by Champion Orangepark Dexter (owned by Mr. and Mrs. Wilton Meyer)—it seemed time to start looking for an old farm to house the growing family. A good location west of Billings, with a creek, several outbuildings, and lots of room for the dogs to run was located; and after much cleaning, scrubbing, hauling, remodeling, and fence mending, the former dairy farm/hog ranch became Beartooth Kennels. The dairy barn became the main kennel building, the heated machine shed a puppy area, the bunkhouse a heated whelping kennel, and the corrals became exercise yards. A new building connected to the house has been recently added. It will house fifteen indoor-outdoor runs, a dog training area, and Byron's art studio.

Byron paints and sculpts in many media and has produced such fine art as a metal fish, a stone cowgirl, and a huge wooden Basset mama with pups that sits in the Wisners' living room. He designs their own Christmas cards each year, Carole's kennel note paper, and her needlepoint.

Beartooth's breeding program has been built on the original Margem Hills, Nancy Evans, Slippery Hill, and Orangepark lines, with the most recent additions being from the Jagersven Kennels. Effort has been made to keep lines separate in some instances, with crossing into various pedigrees within their kennel when it has seemed called for or necessary. Twenty-eight Beartooth Bassets have finished their championships as of April 1984.

Beartooth's main stud force consists of a four-generation father-son family: American and Canadian Champion Beartooth Victor, his son Champion Beartooth Raymond, Raymond's son Champion Beartooth Toby, and Toby's son Champion Beartooth Adrian. Victor, who was Number Three Basset in 1977; Number One Basset, Number Six Hound, and Number Twenty-five among all breeds in 1978; Number Two Basset in 1979; and Number One Basset and Number Nine Hound in 1980, has accumulated fifteen Bests in Show and has nine champion offspring to date.

Other stud dogs figuring prominently in the Wisners' breeding program are Champion Beartooth Karl from the Jagersven background and Champion Beartooth Geronimo from the Orangepark lines.

The Wisners' summer evenings usually include a three-mile jog up the road past the cornfield, puppy feedings, and a practice session with the dogs being currently shown. During the day the dogs are attended by two kennel assistants while Byron attends to his oral surgery practice and Carole teaches music.

Ch. Blue Billy Bojangles, ROM, the all-time Top Producing Basset in the history of the breed. Owned by Diane Malenfant and Claudia Lane, Beaujangle Bassets.

Beaujangle

The Beaujangle Bassets are a joint project, owned by Diane Malenfant and Claudia Lane at Glendale, Arizona. The success of this kennel is a notable one, and the owners tell us with pride that all of their dogs are owner-handled.

The foundation stud at Beaujangle Kennels is Champion Blue Billy Bojangles, ROM. As of May 7th 1984, he has produced a total of 49 American champions, making him the *all-time* top producing Basset in the history of the breed.

Another foundation stud at this kennel is Champion Bar-B Buckets O'Sullivan, ROM, with twelve United States champions to his credit.

Among the bitches, the foundation dams include Champion Beaujangle's Edith Egghead. A current excellent producing bitch is Champion Beaujangle's Camellia.

Champion Beaujangle's Ten is the pioneer Best in Show winner from this kennel, and he has as well numerous Specialty wins to his credit. Additionally, he is a Register of Merit sire.

Belyn

Belyn Bassets, owned by Ben and Carolyn Bolch, are located at High Rolls, New Mexico, and have gained prestige and fame throughout the Basset world through the excellence of their remarkable homebred dog (co-bred with Diane Malenfant), American and Canadian Champion Belyn's Roustabout.

America's Top Basset, 1981-1983, Am. and Can. Ch. Belyn's Roustabout, in a most handsome pose. Owned by Carolyn Bolch, Belyn Bassets, High Rolls, New Mexico. Handled by Judy Webb.

43

"J.R.," as Roustabout is known, first became America's Number One Basset in 1981, repeating the honor in 1982 and 1983. During these years he was also Number Seven Hound in 1981 and Number Five Hound in 1982 and 1983.

Handled by Judy Webb, and shown throughout the country, "J.R." has piled up an imposing record, to say the least. Standing on his score card are twenty all-breed Bests in Show; seventeen Specialty Bests in Show, including two Nationals; 78 firsts in Hound Group; 98 other Group placements; and 243 Bests of Breed.

"J.R." is a son of Champion Blue Hills Bojangles, whose grandparents are Champion Nancy Evans Double Cross, Champion Lindsay's Blissful Bridget, Champion Musicland's Bill Bailey, and, again, Champion Lindsay's Blissful Bridget. "J.R.'s" dam, Belyn's Windflower, goes back to Santana-Mandeville Tarzan and Champion Orangepark Dexter, among others, and thus combines some of America's most successful Basset bloodlines.

"J.R." is a dog in whom to take pride—a great personality as well as a super show dog.

Branscombe

Branscombe Bassets, at Riverton, Illinois, are owned by Francis and Ruth Paule who, as Basset breeders for about fifteen years, have been committed to the principle of one standard and bringing the field and conformation Bassets back together. A second belief is in the Basset's versatility in other activities. Starting in 1974, and now with six generations of "all-rounders," they have annually brought Tracking entries to the Basset Hound Club of America Nationals, have now trained ten T.D.'s (nine of them still alive), and are working on their eleventh Tracking Dog titlist.

In 1978 the Paules joined with Bill and Anne Lindsay to produce the Basset Hound Club of America film on tracking, and Ruth wrote the instructional booklet, *Tracking With A Basset.*

After earning their T.D.'s, the Paules' young dogs start working in the field on rabbit. If they are ready, they may then start in the show ring. The Paules' goal is the dual championship.

At present these enthusiastic fanciers have Dual Champion Branscombe Troilus, T.D., now retired; and his grandson, Field Champion Branscombe Man of La Mancha, T.D. Mancha is three

Ch. Branscombe Man of La Mancha, T.D. in the field. Bred and owned by Francis and Ruth Paule.

Ch. Branscombe Man of La Mancha, T.D., bred and owned by Francis and Ruth Paule.

Dual Ch. Branscombe Troilus, T.D. in June 1976. Owned by Francis and Ruth Paule.

Ch. Branscombe Dulcinea, T.D., taking Winners Bitch for a 5-point "major" under Len Skolnick at Chain O'Lakes in 1982. Owned by Francis and Ruth Paule.

WINNERS BITCH

PHOTO BY K. BOOTH

years old and has only one show point to go to gain his championship, thus earning three titles in one year and becoming the third Basset ever with a dual championship and a third title. The Skolnick's Slippery Hill Cinnamon, C.D., was the first dual champion and Troilus, the second.

Another Basset owned by the Paules is Field Champion Bugle Bay's Much Ado, C.D., T.D.

Mancha and his sister, Champion Branscombe Dulcinea, T.D., (pointed in the field) are both producing champions in the show ring to complete their all-round efforts. Dulcinea's first litter, by Champion Belyn's Roustabout, are all being shown. Champion Branscombe Comte Richlieu and Champion Branscombe Comtesse Andrea, both owned by the Mendelsons in San Francisco, are already finished. Mancha's offspring include a Tracking Dog in the United States, a South African champion and Group winner (Branscombe Neptune), and several youngsters currently in the ring and in the field in the United States and in Canada.

By now, with six generations to demonstrate the possibility, the Paules see an increasing number of people handling their own Bassets in performance activities as well as in the show ring. There also has appeared some interest on the part of field-trialers in improving the conformation of their field-bred Bassets. In 1983 the Lindsays and Francis Paule were responsible for the production of the Basset Hound Club of America film on Basset field trialing, aimed at interesting people in this activity with their Bassets.

Champion Branscombe Man of La Mancha, T.D., was born September 22nd 1980 and was bred by his owners. He is a son of Champion Ramblebriar's Local Broker (Forest Bay Brother Jonathan ex Champion Romansway Ingenue) and Champion Branscombe Bianca, T.D. (Dual Champion Branscombe Troilus, T.D., ex Field Champion La Z Dee J's Bonny Bell).

Dual Champion Branscombe Troilus, T.D., is by Champion Slippery Hill Rudyard (Orangepark Dwight ex Slippery Hill Tamale) from Field Champion La Z Dee J's Bonny Bell (Rebel's Yell ex Nancy Evans Lolita Montez).

The Paules mention that Ray and Louise Wells, of North Harwich, Massachusetts, are other breeders active in both field and conformation, and they have developed several dual champions. Marjorie and James Cook, of Azle, Texas, have also developed multi-title conformation holders in conformation, obedience, and tracking.

Brasstax

Brasstax Bassets at Stony Brook, New York, are owned by Gloria Seifman.

Top dog here is the noted Champion Brendans Brian Boru, who was Number Three Basset for 1983 under the *Canine Chronicle* Routledge Point System ratings.

During 1983, "Geordie," as he is known, won three Specialty Bests of Breed (Long Island Basset Hound Club, Potomac Basset Hound Club, and Charter Oak Basset Hound Club), plus first in seven Hound Groups, second in another seven, third in ten Groups, and fourth in seven more.

Ch. Jercat's Cushie Butterfield, by Ch. Tal-E-Ho's Hot Diggity ex Ch. Jercat's Ballou, completed title at 10 months and gained all points from the puppy classes. In a limited "specials" career has 3 Best of Opposite Sex awards already to her credit. Owned by Brasstax Bassets. Handled by Brian and Nancy Sheehan Martin.

1984 has started off well, too, for this handsome dog, who at less than halfway through the year was Best of Breed at the Kentuckiana Basset Hound Club Specialty, has won three Groups, six additional Group placements, and seventeen Bests of Breed. He is handled by Nancy Sheehan Martin.

"Geordie" was born January 21st 1980 and was bred by John F. and Gwen McCullagh. He is a son of Champion Halcyon Crackerjack (Champion Halcyon Lumberjack ex Jagersven Marchesa) from Champion Brendan's Virginia of Tara (Champion De-Alo's Herman ex Henderson's Bucaneer Bounty).

There is a young bitch at Brasstax who will be one of the foundation bitches for future generations. This is Champion Jercat's Cushie Butterfield, who completed her title in three months' time beginning when only seven months old and entirely from the Puppy Class, gaining her final five-point major under judge Bill Barton.

Cushie should prove a valuable addition to the Brasstax breeding programs, representing as she does some very outstanding bloodlines. She is sired by Champion Tal-E-Ho's Hot Diggity (by American and Canadian Champion Tal-E-Ho's Prancer ex Tal-E-Ho's Bubbles) from Champion Jercat's Ballou (by Champion Hallmark Malcolm ex his daughter, Kimo's Hallejuah).

Bugle Bay

Bugle Bay Bassets, owned by Jim and Margery Cook at Azle, Texas, have some truly remarkable accomplishments to their credit in every facet of the Basset world.

The Cooks have been involved with Bassets since 1965, taking a real interest in conformation, obedience, tracking, and the field. They feel, quite rightly, that the Basset's versatility makes this a really great breed, able to participate successfully in so many areas.

Among the famous dogs at Bugle Bay Kennels are Champion Le Claire's Merry Madelyn, U.D., who was the Cooks' first champion. A daughter of Champion Barbara's J.P. Morgan Le Claire from Hartshead Magnolia, she was only the third Basset ever to attain her combined championship and Utility Dog degree. Her daugher, Champion Bugle Bay's Souffle, U.D., was the fourth. Souffle was an excellent obedience competitor, attaining High in Trial on nine occasions. She

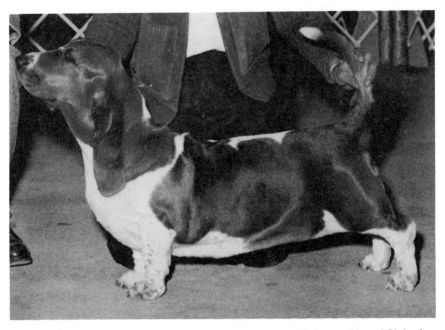

Ch. Bugle Bay's Fondue, C.D., T.D., was High in Trial at the Basset Hound Club of America National in Dallas, 1980. The following day she won her tracking dog title. Fondue is also one of the field dogs at Bugle Bay Kennels, owned by Jim and Margery Cook.

also had 39 points toward an obedience trial championship and was field pointed. Her veteran years were spent field trialing, and she loved every moment of it. In obedience she was always very lively, performing with gusto. Souffle's sire was Champion Lane's Arlo of Castlereach. Her accomplishments, and those of her dam are all the more remarkable because at the time of writing only five Bassets ever have attained both bench championship and U.D. degree.

Another of Madelyn's offspring, Champion Bugle Bay's Ado Annie, C.D., is the dam of Champion Bugle Bay's Bouillon, C.D.X., T.D., ROM, with field points as well.

The Cooks are active in numerous organizations in their area, including the Fort Worth Kennel Club, the Texas Tri-Cities Obedience Club, the Dal-Tex Basset Hound Club, the Basset Hound Club of Greater Fort Worth, and, of course, the Basset Hound Club of America.

Coralwood

Coralwood Bassets at Holmdel, New Jersey, were so named by their owner, William L. Barton, in honor of the section of town in which he and his family lived at the time.

Bill's involvement with Bassets started all the way back in 1956 when his cousin, Jean Williams Watts, then a captain in the Air Force Nursing Corps stationed in California, purchased a beautiful tricolor bitch from the Nelsons, owners of Santana-Mandeville Kennels. This was Miss Clancy of Canoga Park, by Champion Huey of Cypress ex Darwin's Blondie II.

Eventually Jean Watts became increasingly interested in the breed and decided that she would like to have a litter from Clancy. The lovely solid red champion Newtons Imperial was selected for the occasion (by Champion Long View Acres Uncle Ed ex Newtons Tina Maria) and a litter of six was produced, at least two of which finished, one of them Champion Sir Angus of Reno. When the puppies were about eight weeks old, Jean received orders to go overseas and thus became unable to continue her interest with the Bassets. She sold all but her favorite puppy to whom she was especially attached, and Clancy re-

Ch. Coralwood's Without-A-Doubt, by Ch. Abbot Run Valley Crackerjack ex Ch. Abbot Run Valley Perdita, winning Best of Breed at the Rancocas Valley Basset Hound Club Specialty in conjunction with Trenton K.C. in 1968. Owned by William L. Barton.

Ch. Abbot Run Valley Crackerjack, by Ch. Abbot Run Valley Prankster ex Abbot Run Valley Sassy, finishing his title in May 1965 under the late judge Raymond Beale. An outstanding showman, this dog acquired many Best of Breed and Group placements. Owned by William L. Barton.

mained with her parents. Bill Barton was breeding Beagles at the time and had excellent kennel facilities, so he was elected to keep the puppy for Jean until her return home.

One day while out walking this Basset pup, Bill was stopped by someone who commented on the puppy's excellence and asked if Bill had ever considered showing him. He hadn't even an idea then what dog shows were all about; but this puppy met all the requirements for entry, so Bill obtained the necessary form and instructions on how to proceed from there.

Bill Barton's first show as an exhibitor was Monmouth County in 1960 where his dog, whom he had named Mr. Tandy of Coralwood, took second (winning a red ribbon and a small trophy) to a far better behaved puppy, so Bill was not unhappy. Later he learned that his competition that day had been handled by Chrissy Boutell, daughter of the late Clip and Helen Boutell of the Double B Kennels in Connecticut. Following the judging, Bill was told that his dog had great potential to become a champion, but that to accomplish this he would have to educate himself about the procedures of handling and good presentation.

This was the beginning of an enthusiasm that spread to the entire Barton family, especially to daughter Sally, who became a top-grade Junior Handler. Sally became a tremendous help in training and grooming, to all of the Coralwood dogs.

All the Bartons joined a handling class, starting to learn together. Ten months later they returned to the ring, and within eight shows Tandy had become the first of their eleven champions.

In April 1963 the Bartons purchased a young red and white male, Abbot Run Valley Crackerjack, from Walter and Marjorie Brandt of the famous Abbot Run Valley Kennels in Providence, Rhode Island. Seven months old, he was by Champion Abbot Run Valley Prankster ex Abbot Run Valley Sassy. Then three months later, again from the

Ch. Coralwood's Kadiddlehopper, by Ch. Abbot Run Valley Crackerjack ex Miss Mandelene of Coralwood, here is retiring the Frank Hardy Memorial Trophy by going Best of Opposite Sex at the Basset Hound Club of America Specialty in October 1972. Owned by William L. Barton, Coralwood Bassets. This Basset became Top Winning Basset Bitch and No. 7 Basset for 1971, Phillips System.

Brandts, a tricolored year-old bitch was added to Coralwood, Abbot Run Valley Anita, by Champion Abbot Run Valley Brassy ex Champion Abbot Run Valley Gem. Crackerjack finished and then Anita was bred to him, producing five splendid puppies. From this breeding a lovely red and white bitch was kept whom the Bartons named Pearl, the intention being to use her to establish Coralwood's future line. Little did they anticipate that Pearl, now a champion, would be unable to conceive and that Anita would develop internal complications.

But, not discouraged, the Bartons purchased a red and white bitch from Nancy Lindsay of the famed Lime Tree Kennels (Bassets and Bloodhounds). She was named Richard's Ann of Lime Tree, her parents being Champion Lime Tree Micawber and Champion Richardson's Autumn Fire. This bitch, bred to Champion Mister Tandy of Coralwood, produced Miss Mandelene of Coralwood, who later was bred to Crackerjack producing what Bill Barton considers to be one of the most elegant and best moving bitches shown during the later 1960's and early 1970's—an opinion with which the judges obviously agreed as she established one of the most outstanding show records, becoming in 1971 the Number One bitch and the Number Ten Basset—Champion Coralwood's Kadiddlehopper.

When Bill's cousin Jean returned, she did not have the heart to take Tandy back after all that Bill had done with him. Instead, she fell in love with and accepted in replacement a solid red litter-sister to Kattie.

For nineteen years the Bartons bred Bassets. Bill gives special credit to Mr. and Mrs. Walter Brandt for their conscientious breeding program which has contributed so greatly to his own. The Brandts were instrumental in helping him to establish a uniform breeding program, teaching him the importance and effects it would have on future generations.

In 1971, Bill was approved by the American Kennel Club to judge Bassets and Bloodhounds, to which he since has added seven other Hound breeds. In 1975 he became the first American judge to officiate at a Basset Hound Specialty in Germany, at the International Dog Show held at Munich. Then in 1976 he judged the Austrian Basset Hound Specialty in conjunction with the World Dog Show at Innsbruck. These assignments were especially exciting, as they afforded Bill the opportunity to take greetings from our Basset Hound Club overseas and to discuss the breed with fanciers there. He found the people in Europe eager to learn and to know what fanciers in the United States are doing.

Ch. Josephine of Cotton Hill, a granddaughter of Ch. Belbay Wizard, was bred by Priscilla Smith and belongs to Elizabeth W. Redmond. Pictured completing title at Great Barrington handled by Carlton Redmond, August 1959.

Cotton Hill

Cotton Hill Kennels, now located in North Hampton, New Hampshire, were founded in 1957 by Carlton and Elizabeth Redmond. Josephine, their foundation bitch, a red and white, was originally purchased solely as a pet. However, her Belbay lineage, soundness, and temperament attracted the attention of a Dalmatian breeder-friend who encouraged the Redmonds to show her.

Josephine went Best Puppy in Match at an all-breed match under judge Mrs. Nicholas Demidoff. This occasion was Josephine's first outing. Always owner-handled, Josephine finished her championship in five consecutive shows, including a Best of Breed and a Best of Opposite Sex over Specials.

The Redmonds felt that Josephine was worthy of breeding, so they contacted Mrs. M. Lynwood Walton of Lyn Mar Acres fame, who invited them, along with Josephine, to visit the Lyn Mar Acres Bassets. Under Mr. and Mrs. Walton's guidance, a breeding program was started. Josephine's only litter was sired by Lyn Mar Acres De March

Ch. Xaviera of Cotton Hill, taking **Best of Winners** at Carroll K.C. in 1978. Handled by Joy S. Brewster. Owned and bred by Elizabeth W. Redmond.

(Champion Lyn Mar Acres Top Brass ex Champion Debbie's Gift). In it she produced Champion Erminetrude of Cotton Hill. The latter was bred back to her sire, Lyn Mar Acres De March, producing Champion Hello Dolly of Cotton Hill.

Dolly's only litter was sired by Lyn Màr Acres Gold Brick, a De March son, producing Champion Gold Digger of Cotton Hill.

Gold Digger was bred to Champion Lyn Mar Acres End Man, a Champion M'Lord Batuff son, producing her first champion, Limavady's Bill of Cotton Hill, owned by Edmund Hammond. Bill had numerous Bests of Breed to his credit and had sired only two litters with several champions in each when a severe disc problem, requiring surgery, cut short his show career and his use as a stud—surely a pity and one of the disappointments that may come in breeding dogs!

For her second litter, Gold Digger was bred to Lyn Mar Acres Lord Hyssop, also a Batuff son, giving Cotton Hill its next champion, Cristina of Cotton Hill. Bred to Champion Lyn Mar Acres Extra Man (son of Champion Lyn Mar Acres End Man), Christine produced the most recent Cotton Hill champion, Xaviera of Cotton Hill. Before she had even produced one litter it became necessary for Xaviera to be spayed, another disappointment for the Redmonds.

From the beginning, Cotton Hill's policy has been to remain a very small operation, keeping only the pick bitch in each generation and selling the others with a spay agreement. By so doing it was hoped to improve, if only a little, with each champion. All Cotton Hill champions have been homebred and for the most part owner-handled.

With their breeding program temporarily halted following Xaviera, the Redmonds, with the help and kindness of Mr. and Mrs. Frank Kovalic of Stoneybluff Kennels, Milford, Michigan, are continuing their breeding program. It is hoped that Cotton Hill's record of at least one champion in each generation will remain intact.

Ch. Christine of Cotton Hill, bred and owned by Elizabeth W. Redmond, handled by Carlton Redmond; and Ch. Limavady's Bill of Cotton Hill, bred by Elizabeth W. Redmond, owner-handled by Edmund P. Hammond, under judge Mrs. M. Lynwood Walton. Best of Breed and Best of Opposite Sex respectively at Cape Cod February 1976.

Courtside

Courtside Basset Hounds were started in 1962 by former active Boxer enthusiasts, Dr. and Mrs. Phillip L. Fellman, at that time residents of Long Island, now living at Pompano Beach, Florida.

The Fellmans selected a lovely bitch as their foundation, purchased from the Lime Tree Kennels belonging to Mrs. Nancy Lindsay, this bitch a daughter of the notable Champion Lime Tree Micawber. After showing her for awhile and getting her started toward championship, the Fellmans decided that she should be bred to Marjorie Brandt's famed sire Champion Abbot Run Valley Brassy. She was, and in the Fellmans' first Basset litter she presented her owners with a puppy who became famous as a champion in three countries: American, Canadian, and Bermudian Champion Courtside Gorgeous Gussie.

It is interesting that the Fellmans, whose entire family enjoys playing tennis and whose kennel was situated alongside their private tennis court, selected the very appropriate name of Courtside for this kennel; in keeping with this kennel name, each of the Bassets was named for a well-known tennis star. In Gussie's case, she was the namesake of Gussie Moran who made lace panties famous at Wimbledon.

For Gussie's first litter, she was bred to Champion Abbot Run Valley Prankster, from which she produced Champion Courtside Peaches. This was the last litter by Prankster. Peaches was a small, elegant bitch with a truly exceptional head. She did considerable winning and proved a true asset to her owners.

Gussie also produced Champion Courtside For Pete's Sake, the result of a breeding back to her sire, Brassy.

Courtside Bassets were especially active during the late 1960's and early 1970's, producing and showing a goodly number of winners. One of the most consistent of the Fellmans' dogs was a Brassy son bred by Isabel and George Watson whom they purchased as his breeding fit in so exactly with their own program. This was Champion Webbridge Banner Bound, a dog whom Patricia Fellman was especially happy to own as she admired so many things about him. He won just about every Basset Specialty in the East and Midwest during the year he was being really campaigned, and he placed in numerous Groups, earning himself a position among the Top Ten Bassets and culminating his career with an all-breed Best in Show at the Bermuda Kennel Club. Among Patricia's favorites that "Bounder," as this dog

Am., Can., Bda. Ch. Courtside Gorgeous Gussie, famous homebred winning bitch owned by Patricia Fellman, Courtside Bassets. Gussie was from the Fellmans' very first Basset litter, by a noted winner and highly successful producer.

Ch. Courtside For Pete's Sake, one of the splendid winning Bassets owned by Patricia Fellman. Handled by Bobby Fowler.

Am., Can., and Bda. Ch. Courtside Peaches. Handled by Dorothy Hardy for Patricia Fellman, now of Pompano Beach, Florida.

was known, produced was the lovely bitch Courtside Francoise, C.D., who was given to a friend when she lacked just one major and then taken to California and just never made it back to shows again.

Dorothy Hardy handled the Fellman Bassets and was a good friend, a lady from whom Patricia mentions she learned a great deal about Bassets. Then Bobby Fowler took over, handling some Dachshunds as well for the Fellmans.

When Patricia started to judge, the Fellmans decided to go into field trialing instead of the conformation shows with their Bassets, having a marvelous time participating in, "what Bassets are really bred to do," as Patricia puts it. She feels that better understanding of this has helped her in her judging, too.

A comment Patricia makes in closing her kennel story should be of interest and value to our readers. She notes: "I believe they showed them heavier then (in the old dogs' day) than they do now, and feel that the Bassets today have improved in length of neck, (perhaps because we are keeping weight off) and heads are better, but there is lack of bone today."

Halcyon

Halcyon Hounds have been excitingly represented at dog shows during the early 1980's by a most outstanding and excellent dog, Champion Halcyon Crackerjack, ROM, who was bred by Lamont and Vicki Steedle of Virginia and is owned by Gwen McCullagh and Ed Smizer, both of New Jersey.

Shortly after receiving the Best in Specialty Show award at the 1983 Basset Hound Club of America National, "C.J.," as Crackerjack is known to friends and admirers, was retired from active competition with some very noteworthy achievements to his credit. He is the only Basset to win the Canadian National and the American National Specialties both in the same year. He finished his championship with a Specialty Best of Breed from the classes, going on to a total of 22 Specialty Bests of Breed. His total of Best of Breed wins stands at more than 200, plus he has garnered more than 50 Group placements.

Born in 1978, Crackerjack is a son of Champion Halcyon Lumberjack from Jagersven Marchesa. He is recognized by the Basset Hound Club of America's Register of Merit as a top-producing stud, having sired eighteen champions to date with more who are already pointed. Among his offspring are several who themselves are Specialty winners. He has won the Stud Dog Class at the last three National Specialties.

Although Crackerjack is mostly retired now, he still will continue to make occasional ring appearances, handled, as always, by co-owner Ed Smizer.

Het's

Het's Basset Hounds, owned by Hettie Page Garwood at Spicewood, Texas, were established late in the 1950's and are famous in the dog show world as the home of Champion Glenhaven's Lord Jack, ROM, who was the Top Hound of all breeds in the United States for 1971.

Lord Jack's show record was impressive. Shown to his title by Roy Murray, he was later taken out as a Special under Walt Shellenbarger's handling and ran up a list of wins which totaled five all-breed Bests in Show, seven Specialty Bests in Show, 28 times Best Hound, and 138 times Best of Breed.

Sparingly bred, Lord Jack was the sire of some twenty champions and other title-holders in conformation, obedience, and the field. He

Am., Can., Dom., Col., Ven. Ch. Concho's Don Juan, by Am. Ch. Glenhaven's Butcher Boy ex Ch. Manor Hill Greta, was bred by Carol Friend, owned in the U.S. by Hettie Page Garwood, owned and shown in South America by Carmen Benitez. Handled by Richard Guevara. A Best in Show winner in three countries.

has the distinction, at eleven years of age, of winning the 1978 Specialty Show of the Basset Hound Club of Corpus Christi Specialty, where he was owner-handled.

Lord Jack's pedigree reads like a veritable *Who's Who* among Basset Hounds. His sire, Champion Nancy Evans Sir Galahad, was a grandson of Champion Chevalier's Gun Smoke (Champion Belbay Chevalier ex Champion La Belle Penelope of Belleau), Champion Bassett's Barry De Belleau (Champion Rossingham's Narrister ex Bassett's Potiron De Belleau), and Champion Belleau's Venus Del Fairfield (Champion Belleau's Davy Crockett ex Desdemona). His dam, Little Tear Drops, was by American and Bermudian Champion Sir Tomo of Glenhaven, whose dam was Champion Lyn Mar Acres Fyre Ball (Champion Lyn Mar Acres Clown ex Champion Headline of Lyn Mar Acres), and Little Tear Drops was from Eleandon's Happy Times, by a son of Champion Lyn Mar Acres Scalawag from Champion Eleandon's Gypsey.

Ch. Het's Lord Browning, by Het's Frederic ex Ch. Mu Lu's Banana Blossom, is a Lord Jack grandson. Winners Dog at the Basset Hound Club of America National Specialty at Dallas, Texas. Handled by Judy Webb for owner Hettie Page Garwood.

Born in 1967, Lord Jack lived to be fourteen years of age. His breeders were Alan and Dorothy Turner.

Hettie Garwood has owned or bred a great many other noted Bassets who have kept her kennel consistently in the limelight over the past 25 years. One such noted Basset is American, Canadian, Dominican, Colombian, and Venezuelan Champion Concho's Don Juan was sired by Lord Jack, owned and finished in the United States by Hettie. He was then sold to Carmen Benitez for whom he was campaigned in South America by the noted international judge Richard Guevara, who was at that time a handler; Don Juan became a Best in Show winner in three countries in South America. American and Canadian Champion Het's Barney of Whiteside, a son of Lord Jack, has done some exciting winning, including in Specialty competition. Champion Het's Lord Browning is another Lord Jack descendant (grandson) who has won well. And there are many others who have kept, and are continuing to keep, this enthusiastic breeder's banner in the limelight.

Ch. Honeytree's Teddy Bear relaxing at home wearing one of his favorite hats. Mike and Suzy Holm's famed Best in Show dog.

Honeytree

Honeytree Bassets are owned by Mike and Suzy Holm of Buffalo, Minnesota, and are based on foundation stock from Musicland Kennels by way of Champion Musicland's Casey Jones.

The Holms bred their bitch, Honeytree's Peppermint Patty, to Champion Musicland's Houdina, resulting in a stunning Basset dog now famous as a Best in Show and multiple Hound Group winner. This is Champion Honeytree's Teddy Bear, who has been first in the Hound Group on six occasions, second in the Group twelve times, third ten times, and fourth nine times. Additionally he has 56 Best of Breed ribbons, and a Best in Show, although shown on a limited basis. Stan Flowers is his handler.

Honeytree was established in 1977, but Mrs. Holm as a teenager (Suzy Fisher) did raise and show Bassets of her own from 1961 to 1967. Suzy's family owned the Jabal Kennels (her mother's famous Beagle, Champion Johjean's Jabal, was a multi Best in Show winner and Top 15″ Beagle for 1963), and Suzy bred and owned Champion Jabal's Tiger Lily who won the Fort Dearborn Basset Specialty Show. in 1963, Don Sandberg handling.

Most of the Holms' energy these days is spent on Teddy Bear, but they are also starting to show a son of his, and a really nice grandson. The latter, Briarpatch T. Honeytree, gained points at his first show from the Puppy Class. Also there are two Basset litters, grandchildren of Teddy, coming along that look especially promising.

Beagles share the interest at Honeytree.

Jagersven

Jagersven Bassets were started in 1961 with the purchase of Jagersven Samantha by Finn and Mary Louise Bergishagen of Union Lake, Michigan, from Chris Teeter's Long View Acres Kennels. Samantha completed her championship and then was bred to Champion Seifenjagenheim Dominoe, a breeding which produced Champion Jagersven Gigi, who was best of Opposite Sex from the classes at the Basset Hound Club of America Specialty in 1966.

When bred to Champion Lyn Mar Acres Press Agent, Gigi produced three champions: Jagersven Mariner, Monarch II, and Mimi. Monarch was sold as a puppy to the Kovalics and subsequently pro-

Ch. Jagersven Blue Banner, Best of Breed at the Basset Hound Club of America National Specialty in 1978 from the Veteran Bitch Class, the first time a Veteran bitch has won and the first bitch to win the Specialty in 13 years. Finn and Mary Louise Bergishagen, breeders-owners.

Ch. Jagersven Benchmark, by Ch. Stoneybluff Freckles ex Ch. Jagersven Blue Ribbon, born July 1975. The sire of 6 American Champions, 7 Canadian Champions and a Danish Champion. Bred and owned by Finn and Mary Louise Bergishagen.

Am. and Can. Ch. Shadows Snow White, the black bitch purchased in 1970, by Am. and Can. Ch. Gin Dic's Bit O'Brass ex Northwood's Lazy Lizzy. She is the dam of six champions. Bred by James and Carol Schadt. Finn and Mary Louise Bergishagen, owners.

duced six champions when bred to two of their bitches. Mimi was bred to Champion Lyn Mar Acres End Man to produce Jagersven Amos who was the sire of champions for various kennels throughout the country, including Halcyon and Briarcrest.

The kennel name "Jagersven" was registered with the American Kennel Club in 1968. The following year Shadows' Snow White was purchased at a year and a half old and became the foundation bitch for a second and different direction in the kennel's breeding program. She completed her title in just a few shows, all under breeder-judges. In those days a black Basset was extremely rare and created considerable stir. Initially unable to decide on a stud for Snow White, the Bergishagens eventually found one at the National, which they attended at the same time as when they were looking for a stud. He was Champion Margem Hills Mr. Brown, owned by the Williams in Texas. It proved to be a great breeding, producing the three champion bitches, Jagersven Blue Ribbon, Blue Banner, and Blueberry Muffin. Brown had been shipped to the Bergishagens for the breeding to Snow White (reversing the usual custom of shipping the bitch to the dog) and went back home for a short time. He soon returned, however, and remained at Jagersven for the rest of his lifetime. Subsequent breedings produced more champion bitches out of Snow as well as from other champions for other kennels. Brown also produced a tracking titlist. Snow White, as a note of interest, was Best of Opposite Sex at two National Specialties: as a young bitch in 1970 and as a Veteran in 1975.

Champion Jagersven Blue Ribbon was bred to a Snow grandson, Champion Stonybluff Freckles, to produce Champion Jagersven Benchmark. This dog produced six champions in the United States, seven in Canada, and one Danish champion. He is also the grandsire of Champion Halcyon Crackerjack. Champion Jagersven Blue Banner, litter-sister to Blue Ribbon, was Best of Breed from the Veterans Class at the 1978 National, the only Veteran Bitch ever to do so and the first bitch to win the National in thirteen years.

Thirty champions by now have finished at Jagersven, but the dogs mentioned here are, in their owners' opinion, the most memorable and have been the most influential. Others have been bigger winners, but these are the ones who truly contributed the most one way or another.

The Bergishagens have been active in the Basset Hound Club of America for more than twenty years, with Finn serving as President over several terms totaling about seven years. Both are also members of the Detroit Kennel Club.

Joan Urban's Fort Merrill

Joan Urban's first Basset champion was a dog she had purchased as a pet for $35. This dog, who grew up to become Mexican and American Champion Monsieur Pierre La Rue, was whelped in November 1959 and was sired by Champion Felix of Le Chenil ex My Darling Clementine. He was bred by Jean Wylie and lived to the good old age of fourteen years.

Pierre was intended as a pet for the Urbans' three young sons, but Joan became impressed with his quality as he matured and handled him to both his titles. He finished easily, never being out of the ribbons; and although never really campaigned, he was shown several times as a Special and won several Group placements.

In 1966 Joan Urban purchased Champion Nancy Evans Sir Galahad from the Carl Fuhrmanns of San Antonio who had campaigned him to his show record. To her knowledge, Sir Galahad was the first Texan-owned Basset to go Best in Show. His record included 50 Bests of Breed, sixteen Hound Group firsts, eight seconds, six thirds, and seven Hound Group fourths—an impressive record for a Basset at that time. Unfortunately, he produced only three litters. The most noteworthy of his offspring was Champion Glenhavens Lord Jack, owned and loved by Hettie Page Garwood of Spicewood, Texas. Lord Jack was handled to Top Hound All-Breeds in 1971 by Walt Shellenbargar.

In 1969, Joan applied for and was granted approval by the American Kennel Club to judge Bassets. In 1976 she completed the Hound Group, and concurrently she received her B.A. degree from college, being a full time student at the time.

Now all of the Joan Urban Bassets have been placed in good homes except, of course, old Pierre and the lovely bitch, Champion Lyn Mar Acres Plane Fare, purchased from Peg Walton. This bitch was bred to Champion Margem Hills Mr. Brown in 1970 and produced two champion daughters. One of these was Champion Joan's Urban's Etc of Tantivy ("Happy") who was sent to Jane Luce and the Tantivy Basset Pack in Kansas City for one litter. Then later she went to Eric and Erica George at Strathalbyn, where she completed her championship and produced two litters.

When it became necessary, in 1979, for the Urbans to move to Dinero, Texas, to oversee their cattle-ranching operations at Fort Merrill, the Georges were so kind as to send Mrs. Urban two of "Happy's" offspring. These became Champion Joan Urban's

The very famous Ch. Nancy Evans Sir Galahad in a most beautiful head study. Joan Urban, owner, Dinero, Texas.

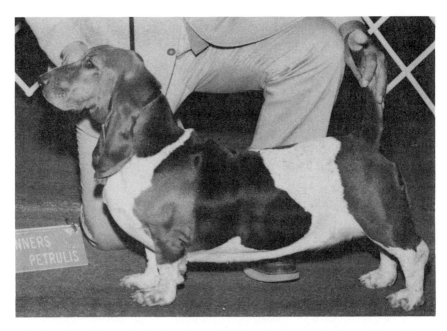

Ch. Fort Merrill Serendipity, born Sept. 1981, bred and owned by Joan Urban. Sired by Strathalbyn Sidhiron ex Strathalbyn Bethshebae.

Strathalbyn Et Al (Electra), sired by the Georges' top winning Champion Strathalbyn Shoot to Kill; and Strathalbyn Spotless, by their Champion Lyn Mar Acres P.B.R. The Georges also sent a "Happy" granddaughter (Strathalbyn Dhaktivadhanta) and a grandson (Champion Strathalbyn Rival) along with several other Bassets stemming from Lyn Mar-Tantivy bloodlines. This gene pool has produced Champion Fort Merrill Nearly Vanilla, Champion Fort Merrill Serendipity (finished in the early 1980's), and Fort Merrill High Trump with nine points including both majors—all owned by Joan Urban; and Fort Merrill Lieutenant, whose thirteen points, as we write, include a major—co-owned by the Salyers and C.R. Fredericksen.

Currently Joan Urban has become deeply involved with the Chinese Shar Pei, serving on the Standards Committee of their parent club as the Chairman. She is one of four members appointed by the Specialty club as a liaison committee to work with the American Kennel Club toward recognition of the Shar Pei, and she is past president of the South Central Chinese Shar Pei Club.

So far as her judging goes, she has just passed her 100th assignment.

Lyn Mar Acres

Lyn Mar Acres Kennels have, since the forties, been in the winners circle with their dogs. Margaret S. Walton, owner of this famed kennel, deserves tremendous credit for the very great impact and influence of her dogs on the development of the breed.

Located at Mt. Holly, New Jersey, Lyn Mar Acres very rightfully can be referred to as a legend in its own time, for it is exactly that. When one thinks back over the dogs produced there and representing Mrs. Walton (usually owner-handled) at the shows, one cannot be other than impressed and filled with very genuine respect and admiration for this lady as a breeder and as an expert on what is and is not desirable in Bassets.

This admiration increases as we study kennel histories, noting how many of the most successful have their roots in Lyn Mar Acres! Mrs. Walton has provided foundation stock for many of the best and must take pride in this fact as she surveys Basset progress around the United States and Canada, in England where Lyn Mar Acres Bassets

Ch. Lyn Mar Acres Press Agent, a multiple Group and Best in Show winner, here is winning the Hound Group following Best of Breed at Susquehanna Basset Hound Speciality in 1965. Bred, owned and handled by Margaret S. Walton. Son of Lyn Mar Acres De March (litter brother to Ch. Lyn Mar Acres Debutante) ex Ch. Lyn Mar Acres Ballyhoo.

have been imported to help maintain quality there, and, in fact, every part of the world where show-type Bassets are known.

Mrs. Walton's own foundation stock is based on Gerald Livingstons' Kilsyth dogs (from the leading English exports during the early days in Bassets) and from the Greenly Hall Bassets, which provided her with a splendid early producer for her kennels in Champion Duchess of Greenly Hall, bred by Frank Kiernan from Mitz and sired by Champion Duke of Greenly Hall.

Through the generations, Lyn Mar Acres has produced a steady succession of great Bassets. We are happy to say that Mrs. Walton, who has become one of our most popular and respected multiple breed judges, is still doing some breeding there, although on a more limited basis, and that the quality of Lyn Mar Acres dogs is still as instantly recognizable in the present generation as in the dogs preceding them.

The following brings you, in Margaret Walton's own words, the story of the beginning of Lyn Mar Acres Basset Hounds. She has told it in so charming a manner that the authors prefer to quote directly rather than follow the usual custom of writing it in our own style.

TIME: Spring 1942

SCENE: Breakfast table at Olden Oak. Husband enters with sporting magazine, places it before unsuspecting wife. Staring into an empty warren is a sorrowful face and at the 'exit' is a grinning fox cub! Friend husband now states that is what he has always wanted since having hunted with one as a boy—wife retorts "not on your life" looking at the crippled forelegs of the puppy.

Thus the hunt was on for a *sound* Basset Hound of type with ability as a gift for the hunter in the family. Nearly a year later, much correspondence having gone out to every known Basset Kennel, I heard from the Foglesons of Greenly Hall Kennels. The provisos were to the point:

IF they could purchase the dam of Duchess of Greenly Hall.

IF we would finish her (she had 5 points)

IF we would breed her carefully

she might be available. We agreed—and waited. Attending the Garden in February 1943—there she sat—all 12 " 40 lbs. of her. We wanted to take her home with us but her famous handler, Lee Wade, had no authority to let her go so the following morning we placed a phone call and the rest is history.

Duchess was our house dog, a good hunter (in 1946 she was BB at Westminster and her litter-sister finished her Fd. Ch.) and

Ch. Lyn Mar Acres Sir Michelob, by Ch. Lyn Mar Acres M'Lord Batuff ex Ch. Lyn Mar Acres Carling (she is a daughter of Ch. Lyn Mar Acres P.T. Barnum) was bred and owned by Mrs. Margaret S. Walton. Handled by Roy Murray.

a great foundation. We followed all suggestions of the Foglesons which led us to Mr. and Mrs. Gerald Livingston of Kilsyth Pack. They had not allowed anyone to breed into their kennels for 15 years but because of the bloodlines carried by Duchess daughter by Ch. Promise of Greenly Hall, we had a litter by Kilsyth Lucky resulting in Clown, Actor (sire of Ch. His Lordship of LMA), Kilsyth Longfellow, Glamour, Charm and two other males. We later were able to purchase the last known male of the Bijou of Banbury pack owned by Mrs. Ford.

We have always maintained the Walhampton bloodlines and, when an outcross was needed, we went to England for it. Our deepest thanks will always go to Irene and Harold Fogleson, Greenly Hall Kennels; Mr. and Mrs. Gerald Livingston, Kilsyth Kennels; Mrs. Consuelo Ford, Bijou of Banbury Pack; and Mr. and Mrs. Andrew Porter of Upland Pack who allowed us to use their lovely English import Hound who was not available to the public. Their early support and advice was highly valued and we trust they would and do approve of our 40 plus years of breeding *sound, typy Basset Hounds* with ability, based on the pattern they all set for us to follow.

73

Manor Hill

Manor Hill Bassets, owned by Ronald and Joan Scholz at Boyton Beach, Florida, were started in the late 1950's when Joan, who had loved dogs all her life, had seen and succumbed to the charms of "Cleo," the famous Basset television star of that period.

Perk's Lady Charm and Perk's Happy Delight, who were sisters, were purchased by Joan after considerable search to locate any Bassets available for sale. These two came from Charles Perkins at Tunkhannock, Pennsylvania, and were daughters of Champion Darwin's Hermanz.

Both of these girls were bred by the Scholzes to Helen Boutell's Champion Double B's Ishmael. After this the Perk bitches were spayed, but Joan kept the best from Happy Delight which Helen Boutell urged her to enter at match shows, getting her interested in the fun of exhibiting dogs. Between 1957 and 1961, Joan went through the purchase of a series of show prospects, none of which proved successful. All were tried out in the ring and for breeding and then spayed following their first litters. However, along the way, Manor Hill Penny Candy was purchased from Helen Boutell and then bred to Champion Lime Tree Micawber. This produced Manor Hill's Dora, and the Scholzes at

Ch. Manor Hill Tooth Fairy, Multi-Group and Specialty winner, Top Basset Bitch in U.S.A. for three years, and Top Producer on the Top Ten Basset Hounds for two years. Dam of 3 U.S.A. champions; a Canadian Ch. and an International Ch. By Ch. Forestbay Montgomery ex Manor Hill Moon Bonnet. Handled by Howard Bygood for Ronald and Joan Scholz.

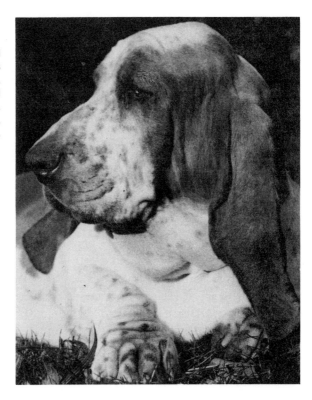

Int. Ch. Manor Hill Yankee Doodle Miss was bred by Joan C. Scholz and is owned by Mr. and Mrs. F. Bennets, Madrid, Spain.

last were on the way to success, as this eventually led to producing Champion Manor Hill Fringe Benefit, a National Specialty winner.

It took a tremendous amount of convincing him to part with her, but eventually the Scholzes were able to purchase Bonnie Ridge Fire-Bird from the late Arthur Fitzsimmons of Long Island, New York. This bitch was a year old at the time of purchase, and it was she who became the true beginning of Manor Hill. Fire-Bird was by Champion Lyn Mar Acres Barrister (Champion His Lordship of Lyn Mar Acres ex Champion Headline of Lyn Mar Acres) from Bonnie Ridge Best Tip (Champion Lyn Mar Acres Brass Band ex Lime Tree Miss Bonnie Ridge, who was by Champion Seifenjagenheim Lazy Bones ex Champion Lyn Mar Acres Zephyr). She was the first dog Joan Scholz showed who ever won a point, and she really proved well worth having waited for, as her first weekend in the ring she won a five-point Specialty major plus two additional points at the companion show. Fire-Bird finished quickly and was bred to Champion Abbot Run Valley Brassy, from which came Champion Doc Floyd of Manor Hill (a Group winner and winner of the spring National Specialty) and

Champion Forget-Me-Not of Manor Hill (the dam of several champions and the first homebred champion for Ronald and Joan Scholz). We understand that Forget Me Not became the foundation bitch for Howard and Blackie Nygood's Bassets and lived for seventeen years "on their couch."

Of course the breeding of Fire-Bird to Brassy was repeated. This time the great Champion Manor Hill Top Spot, ROM, was in the litter, along with the lovely bitch Champion Manor Hill Greta, ROM. Top Spot won the National Specialty himself and produced two others who did likewise, Champion Kazoo's Galloping Gilch and Champion Manor Hill Fringe Benefit. Sadly, Top Spot suffered from a kidney problem which took his life at only four and a half years—what a loss to the breed!

Although she comments that she was not a good handler, Joan Scholz showed all of the aforementioned winning dogs herself, occasionally enlisting the assistance of Alfred J. Murray, a good friend whom she credits with having taught her much about the breed.

Dora, mentioned at the beginning of this story, was bred to Top Spot and produced Champion Manor Hill Fringe Benefit, ROM. Top Spot and Forget-Me-Not along with Fringe Benefit formed the nucleus of Manor Hill's breeding program, while Champion Manor Hill Greta and Champion Manor Hill Doc Floyd went out winning, eventually being sold to Frank Harrison and Mary Jo Shields respectively.

Fire-Bird was bred for a third time to Brassy, thus producing Champion Forestbay Orvil of Manor Hill, ROM, who was purchased as a youngster by Forestbay where he joined the Top Spot and Forget-Me-Not progeny already there and producing well. Orvil's contributions included Forestbay Manor Hill Mahalia, who produced both Champion Forestbay Joshua (by Top Spot) and his son Champion Forestbay Montgomery.

In the mid-sixties, the Scholzes purchased Manor Hill Diane from Sonny Collee. Diane was a Top Spot daughter from Champion Kazoo's Flora Tina and was bred to Fringe Benefit. Champion Manor Hill Lemon Twist came from this litter and became a foundation bitch for Windamohr Kennels, as did the lovely winning bitch, Champion Manor Hill Michelle, with whom Joy Brewster did considerable important winning for the Scholzes and co-owner James A. Grinder.

Joan Scholz credits Diane's influence on the head quality of Manor Hill Bassets, to which she added the length of head and depth of muzzle which Joan felt had previously been lacking.

Ch. Manor Hill Father James, ROM, is the sire of 25 champions to date including two Best in Show sons, Group and Specialty winners. Bred and owned by Joan and Ronald Scholz, Manor Hill Bassets.

It was Diane, bred to Blackie's Beemer, who produced not only Champion Manor Hill Moon Dance (purchased and finished by the Howard Nygoods) but also Manor Hill Moon Bonnet. The latter bred to Champion Forestbay Montgomery in turn produced that most gorgeous bitch Champion Manor Hill Tooth Fairy who became Top Winning Basset Bitch over a three-year period in the United States, a multiple Group and Specialty winner, and a Top Producer, *Kennel Review* system. Bonnet and Montgomery also produced Champion Manor Hill Father James, ROM, the sire of 25 champions as we write (with more sure to finish), including two Best in Show sons and Champion Manor Hill Molly Molly, foundation bitch for Redemption Rock Kennels and the granddam of Champion Redemption Rock Zapper.

Tooth Fairy was in every way a very special bitch. She was bred to Champion Tal-E-Ho Prancer (one of Top Spot's famous grandsons) with pick bitch from this litter going to Deirdre Fisher to be used as the foundation for her Canadian kennel, Corkery. Named Manor Hill Sweet Tooth, she finished quickly in Canada and then produced numerous quality champions of her own.

Coralwood's Cousin Kate produced two puppies which Joan Scholz acquired: Windamohr Gamble, sold to Sandra Campbell and Nancy Taylor as a show prospect; and Windamohr's Autumn of Topohil who went for the same purpose to Jean Sheehy. Both have done well, and Gamble is now a best in Show winner.

In addition to her talents and success in the show ring, Tooth Fairy made a notable contribution to Bassets as a producer. We've already mentioned her important Canadian daughter Sweet Tooth, but there were others, too. By Champion Blackie's Beemer she was the dam of Champion Manor Hill Baby Tooth, Champion Manor Hill Pillow Talk, Champion Manor Hill Prime Time, and Manor Hill Ultra Brite. By Father James, her half-brother, she produced International Champion Manor Hill Yankee Doodle Miss, living in Madrid, Spain, where she is owned by the Fred Bennets.

In June 1983, Ronald Scholz took an early retirement and he and Joan are selling their Connecticut home and kennel for, as Joan puts it, "some turn-key-type" quarters which will leave them the freedom to travel, something to which they long have looked forward. The dogs have been placed in good homes where they will continue their lives with loving owners. Joan plans, now, to expand her judging activities, which will be nice as she is a very knowledgeable lady who can be counted on for a most expert job.

My Lu

My Lu Bassets are owned by Louisa A. Myers at Spicewood, Texas, who has done some very good work with her dogs in field and obedience and has successful conformation winners as well.

Champion Hiflite's Big John, T.D., by Champion Glenhaven's Butcher Boy ex Champion Kazoo's Question Mark, was field pointed and was close to his field championship when he died at only nine years age—truly a sad loss for his owner!

My Lu's Sunshine Shirley, C.D., won the Veterans Obedience Class at the National in Dallas in 1982, and with another lovely Basset who is co-owned by Louisa Myers and Het Garwood (second to Shirley in Veterans), Het's Here Comes The General, won the Brace competition as well that day.

Champion My Lu's Brunhilde, daughter of Champion My Lu's Doctor Tom ex My Lu's Cindy, gained championship honors in good competition and is an asset to My Lu Bassets.

Ch. Hiflite's Big John, T.D., by Ch. Glenhaven's Butcher Boy ex Ch. Kazoo's Question Mark. John was field pointed and only lacked a 1st place to complete his field championship when his death at nine years prevented this accomplishment. Owned by Louisa A. Myers.

Northwoods

Northwoods Bassets, a most esteemed and successful kennel founded by Don and Barbara Martin and located at Libertyville, Illinois, is a family project enthusiastically shared by the Martin daughter Heidi and her two brothers, Peter and Bryan.

The Martins had been in Bassets for awhile when, in 1970, a disastrous fire struck. They were then about to finish a dog and a bitch from a breeding with Champion Galway Meshak, owned by Col. Julian and Betty Dexter. Following their great loss to the fire, the Martins were given a three-month-old bitch by the Dexters, Galway Theresa. Peter Martin lost no time in getting her ready for the ring, all lead-trained and ready to go when she reached six months of age. This bitch did splendid winning for the Martins, who eventually sent her East to the Jermans to be bred to their Champion Tal-E-Ho's Prancer.

Just before Theresa's litter was due, the Martins had the opportunity to purchase Champion Tal-E-Ho's Top Banana, whom Donald Martin had judged on the Cherry Blossom Circuit. They did so promptly, and Top Banana became a source of tremendous joy to the entire family. His record was a fabulous one, his admirers almost countless. He was a Basset with whom to reckon in the show ring, and he was a valuable and dominant sire as well.

Ch. Northwood's The Diplomat, by Ch. Tal-E-Ho's Prancer ex Ch. Galway Theresa winning the Veteran Dog Class at the National Specialty in 1983. Bred by Peter C.J. Martin and co-owned by him with Barbara Martin.

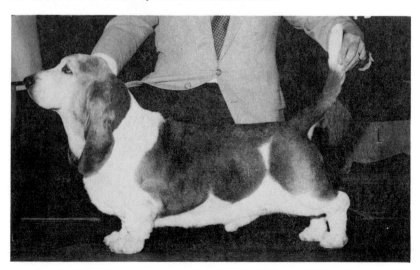

Ch. Tal-E-Ho's Eager Beaver, by Ch. Tal-E-Ho's Top Banana ex Ch. Tal-E-Ho's Scamp, bred by Henry and Ann Jerman, owned by Peter C.J. Martin and Denny and Sherry Neiberger. Easily finished and won breeds. A closely bred excellent producer.

Referring back to the puppies which Theresa had been expecting, her litter included Champion Northwoods The Diplomat, Northwoods Betty O'Windamohr (a bitch sold to Windamohr Kennels in Maryland), and Northwoods Mary Jo (a bitch sold to Hooper-Knolls Kennels in California). Later the Martins bought a great-grand-daughter of Theresa from California, Denmar's Snickers.

When Theresa was bred again, it was to Top Banana. Northwoods Banana Peal was in this litter, the first of "Topper's" 27 champions.

The Jermans used Top Banana on several occasions with their bitches at Tal-E-Ho; and from the second breeding of Tal-E-Ho Scamp to him, the Martins purchased Tal-E-Ho's Eager Beaver. Donald Martin comments, "With the exception of Top Banana, Beaver is my favorite—a smaller edition of his sire, with the great personality and loyalty."

Barbara Martin's sudden death a few years ago was a sad loss not only to her family but also to the entire Basset Fancy. Never could there be a more enthusiastic and dedicated Basset lover than was this charming lady. Fortunately her husband and children have retained their interest in the breed. In fact, their ranks were fortified when, in 1982, son Bryan married Nancy Sheehan who also is very much "into" Bassets.

Notrenom

Notrenom Bassets were established back in 1950 when Richard and Evelyn Bassett from, in those days, Woodinville, Washington, started their involvement with the breed.

The first two Basset Hounds purchased by these fanciers were from Franklin W. Jones, who had Upland stock at Fairfax, Virginia. These were a dog and a bitch, Champion Jones' Virginia Jim and Champion Jones' Virginia Jean. In addition to gaining his championship in conformation, Jim also earned a C.D. title, only the third Basset in this country to have accomplished this.

Jim promptly proved his value as a stud dog when Bonny's Cissy Sue (from Hartshead and Greenly Hall strains) was bred to him with the resulting litter including future champion Mattie's Quercus, C.D. The latter sired thirteen champions.

Sir Hubert II, a double grandson of Hartshead Pepper, was chosen as the stud for Jean, which also proved a sensible decision. They produced Champion Basset's Jody and Josephine. Jody carried on the family tradition by producing Champion Bassett's Miss Wrinkles; and Josephine became the dam of Champion Bassett's Roustabout, winner of seven Bests in Show and 34 Hound Groups, along with siring eight champions.

Rossingham Barrister was imported by the Bassetts in 1955, from Mrs. Hodson's noted Rossingham Kennels. Making his show debut in the United States in 1956, he promptly won the Hound Group. Roustabout sired 23 champions, including Champion Bassett's Barry De Belleau, top producing stud in the breed for 1961; and Champion Notrenom's Howsaboutdot, top producing bitch for 1966. Barrister was by English Champion Grim's Doughnut ex English Champion Grim's Pillow.

Based on this solid foundation, the Bassetts have bred an impressive number of outstanding and successful winners over the past decades. It is interesting to note that when they started breeding, they chose to call their dogs "Bassetts Bassets" as their kennel identification, but somewhere along the way came the A.K.C.'s decision that breed names could not be used for kennel identification. I am sure that anyone even vaguely familiar with the French language realizes that "Notrenom" (a combination of two French words) translates into "Our name" in English, which we think made an ideal identification for the Bassetts' magnificent hounds!

Ch. Galway's Patrick in May 1969, bred by Mrs. Julian S. Dexter, and owned by Mr. and Mrs. Richard Bassett. A lemon and white son of Ch. Abbot Run Valley Brassy, Patrick was handled by Mr. Bassett to a Best of Breed win under Marjorie Siebern.

Three generations of Basset Hounds at Richard and Evelyn Bassett's noted kennel: Ch. Mattie's Quercus, C.D., Ch. Bassett's Jody, Ch. Bassett's Miss Wrinkles, and Ch. Bassett's Dark Delite, from the 1950's-1960's. All famous winners of their time.

Slippery Hill Quixote, ROM, a Top Producer, winning the Rancocas Basset Hound Club Specialty in 1970. Bobby Barlow handled for Leonard Skolnick, Slippery Hill Bassets.

Slippery Hill

Slippery Hill Bassets, owned by Dr. and Mrs. Leonard Skolnick and now located at Harwood, Maryland, came into being as the result of Dr. Skolnick's purchase of his first Basset in 1956 and his first litter of the breed, by this dog, in 1961.

Dr. Skolnick, at the time a professor of chemical engineering, acquired his first Basset, whom he called "Boris" (more formally named Hunting Horn Hermes), prior to his and Marge's marriage; and Marge admits that in the beginning she was partially afraid of "Boris" because she had been bitten by a dog when she was a child. She was soon won over, however, and enjoyed attending field trials with her future husband. Eventually "Boris" was joined by a bitch named Candy (a daughter of Champion Belbay Xtra Handsome and bred by Norwood Engle). In due time "Boris" and Candy presented Dr. Skolnick with a litter, from which a dog, Sam, and two bitches, Chloe and Pandora, were kept. Chloe was eventually taken to a match show where she met with success and definitely sharpened the Skolnicks' appetite for this type of competition. With the thought in mind of doing some breeding, Marge began to study pedigrees, tracing back to the British foundations, and an appreciation of linebreeding started to grow.

Dr. Skolnick purchased a farm in Pennsylvania, and a kennel identifying name was selected—"Slippery Hill" for the one over which the hounds ran in search of rabbits at the farm.

Champion Long View Acres Donna (linebred to Champion Slowpoke Hubertus and to Champion Fanny of En Hu) and Do-Cy-Bo's Deborah, representing Warwick breeding, with roots back to Lyn Mar, were selected for the breeding program, purchased respectively from Mary Jo Shields and from Dorothy Bowers.

Donna was bred to her brother, Champion Do-Cy-Bo's Domino, from which litter Slippery Hill Belinda remained with the Skolnicks. Then, in 1962, an event took place which completely changed the Skolnicks' point of view about the breed and their goals of what was to become their sort of Basset. Dr. Skolnick had by then joined the National (Basset Hound Club of America) and of course the Slippery Hill dogs were entered for the field trial and Specialty. It so happened that Paul and Helen Nelson also attended these events, with some stunning representatives of their Santana-Mandeville dogs, and to the latter the Skolnicks' completely lost their hearts, especially to Champion Gladstone of Mandeville.

The Skolnicks and the Nelsons found that they had many similar ideas regarding Bassets as functional animals as well as about conformation and beauty in the breed, and a warm friendship soon grew between them. It was happy news indeed for the Skolnicks when the Nelsons moved East within a reasonable driving distance from Slippery Hill, making possible many pleasant days spent together.

At this 1962 Specialty, the Nelsons scored a "clean sweep." Gladstone, despite his ten years of age, quite handily won Best of Breed and Santana-Mandeville Olivia took Winners Bitch from the Puppy Class. The Skolnicks were delighted that when the Nelsons returned to California temporarily, Gladstone was sent to them along with two other champions, Minnie and Claude, and several of the Santana-Mandeville youngsters to try out for hunting at Slippery Hill.

The more they saw of them, the more strongly the Santana-Mandeville dogs appealed to the Skolnicks. They became personally acquainted with each and every one of the dogs, particularly following the Nelsons' move to the East, and were quite thoroughly delighted upon their marriage to have the Nelsons offer them any male they might like to have as a wedding gift. This gave the Skolnicks some serious thought, which ended in their selection of Santana-Mandeville Rodney, from Dr. Skolnick's favorite of the bitches, the glorious

Champion Santana-Mandeville Gwendolyn. Rodney, nearly a champion when he came to Slippery Hill, was a small dog, due to which it seemed difficult at first for the judges to recognize his quality. But a young handler with a keen eye saw him and agreed with the Skolnicks regarding his potential. So it was that the association between the Skolnicks and Bobby Barlow was underway, along with a successful career for Rodney that landed him in the Number Three spot for Bassets in 1961 and Number One on the East Coast.

Rodney became the foundation stud at Slippery Hill, several bitches having already been bred to him prior to his departure for the show circuits. However, other bitches were becoming due for breeding, and with Rodney away the Skolnicks felt the need of another stud to be used on their bitches. The Nelsons were beginning to disperse Santana-Mandeville at that time, and it was suggested that the Skolnicks come to look over the dogs. The one who most appealed to them was Santana-Mandeville Egghead, an admiration which was obviously mutual as Egghead never left their side as the Skolnicks toured the kennel. When they left for home, Egghead was with them, despite some faint uneasiness over the fact that he was five years old and had never been bred—unnecessary misgivings as it turned out, as Egghead promptly finished his championship and sired his first litter.

Rodney, meanwhile, had been used for breeding to Belinda, producing a stunning young dog in Champion Slippery Hill Grover, who quickly became a champion for his novice owner H.D. Deffinbaugh, and Slippery Hill Gina.

The Rodney daughters were bred to Egghead with beautifully satisfactory results. From this combination came some lovely Bassets, including Champion Slippery Hill Cinnamon, Paprika, Nutmeg, and the very worthy producing bitch, Tamale.

Tragedy struck in the form of Egghead's sudden death from a stroke when only eight years old—a sad blow indeed for the Skolnicks. Rodney was retired from the show ring to come home so that the Skolnicks could try their breeding plan in reverse—Egghead daughters bred to Rodney, which also worked out well.

Need of a new stud for use on the Egghead-Rodney descendants eventually arose. This led the Skolnicks to William Meyer's handsome dog out on the Coast, Champion Orangepark Dexter, half-brother to Rodney and therefore ideal for the Slippery Hill bitches. Inquiries were made, and the result was an infusion of Dexter and his brother Dwight being introduced to Slippery Hill's breeding program.

Dual Ch. Slippery Hill Cinnamon, C.D., born May 1966, by Ch. Santana Mandeville Egghead ex Slippery Hill Felice, was bred by David K. Barnes. Cinnamon completed her championship in 1967 and her C.D. in 1976. Owner, Leonard Skolnick.

Ch. Slippery Hill Holy Toledo, born 1973, by Ch. Sir Raleigh of Bridi ex Slippery Hill Yolanda, bred and owned by Leonard Skolnick. Co-owner, Byron Wisner.

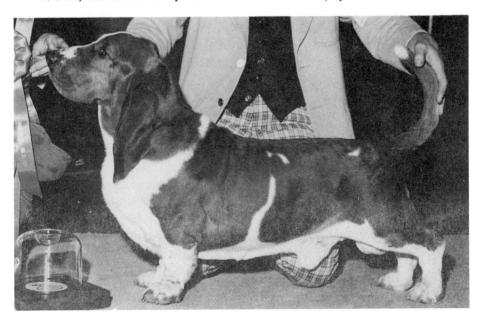

Slippery Hill Quixote was by Dexter from a lovely linebred bitch, Noble Faith's Glint O'Gwendolyn. He was a very handsome and perfectly bred dog for whom the Skolnicks had high hopes. His sudden death of heartworm just short of completion of his championship was a heartbreaker.

Studly von Happy Jack, by Champion Orangepark Dexter ex Slippery Hill Lana; and Slippery Hill Mocha, by Slippery Hill Quixote ex Slippery Hill Katrinka, combined to produce the dog who might well be called a breeder's dream come true, Champion Slippery Hill Hudson. During the 1970's, this splendid dog chalked up a formidable record for Mrs. Alan Robson under Bobby Barlow's handling. Included in his wins were 30 Bests in Show (a record number for a Basset to date, the Skolnicks tell us), several Basset Specialties, America's Number One Hound in 1975, and best of Breed at Westminster 1975-1977. Added to this, Hudson was a successful sire, two of his loveliest daughters being Champion Barmar's Linan-Hugh Cracker, owned by Anna Hughes of Pompton Lakes, New Jersey; and Sanchu's Butterfly, bred and owned by Kitty and Chuck Steidel.

Sharing their interest with the show Bassets are the field dogs and their activities, and Dr. and Mrs. Skolnick note with pride that in addition to more than 30 show champions they have also bred at least 27 field champions, five grand field champions (winners competing in the Champion Stakes at trials), and one dual champion, the latter, Dual Champion Slippery Hill Cinnamon, C.D., having been the first Basset to hold a triple title.

Probably the most exciting single day in the Skolnicks' years with Bassets was the one during 1974 when Champion Slippery Hill Hudson won the Basset Hound Club of America National Specialty and Field Champion Slippery Hill Sophie won the field trial at the same event.

One of the Skolnicks' outstanding field trial hounds was Field Champion Slippery Hill Yours Truly, who gained the Purina Award for Outstanding Field Trial Basset of the Year 1979.

Several Slippery Hill Bassets have been awarded the Basset Hound Club of America Register of Merit for champion producing dogs and bitches. These were show stud Slippery Hill Quixote and field bitches Field Champion Slippery Hill Sophie and her daughter Champion Slippery Hill Prudence, who was honored as the Top Producing Basset Bitch for the year 1982.

The Skolnicks were awarded the Navar's Breeder's Award for breeding the top number of field champions for the years 1976 and 1982.

Ch. Santana
Mandeville
Egghead, owner-
handled by
Leonard Skolnick,
at Delaware
County in 1964.

Ch. Slippery Hill
Nathan Detroit,
handled by Bobby
Barlow for owner,
Leonard Skolnick.

Solitude Creek

Solitude Creek Basset Hounds at Easton, Maryland, belong to Alice B. Lane who deserves great credit for the quality she has bred and thus for her contribution to the breed. Mrs. Lane nowadays is best known and widely admired as a multiple breed judge, but in the past she has been an active breeder-exhibitor of some truly notable Bassets.

It was early in the 1960's that Mrs. Lane was showing her memorable homebred bitch Champion Solitude Creek How Bout That, a daughter of Champion Lyn Mar Acres Press Agent from Solitude Creek Crown Treasure. "Peanuts" gained her title with all major points in 1965 in only four shows: Shawnee Kennel Club where she was Winners Bitch; Potomac Basset Hound Club Specialty where she was Best of Winners; Harford County Kennel Club, again Winners Bitch; and climaxing it all, Winners Bitch, Best of Winners, and best of Opposite Sex over Specials at Trenton.

But that was not all! "Peanuts" was bred to Champion Lyn Mar Acres M'Lord Batuff, and on July 20th 1967 she presented her owner with a litter which included three highly successful champions: American and Canadian Champion Solitude Creek Sophocles, Champion Solitude Creek Sassy Fras, and Champion Solitude Creek Sycamore.

Sophocles easily won his championship in the United States and later was sold to Rosemary McKnight in Canada, who made him a Canadian champion. He became a Top Producer and a Top Hound in Canada.

Sassy, a most flashy and outgoing bitch, also went through to her title with flying colors. Unfortunately, she died in 1975 without having produced a litter although she had been bred twice.

Sycamore, at only ten months of age, went Winners Dog and Best of Winners for a three-point major at the Susquehanna Basset Hound Club Specialty under judge Chris Teeter. Outstanding in type and soundness, he completed his championship at eleven months of age and was Best of Winners each time shown but once. As a Special he gained numerous Bests of Breed.

Opposite page: *(Top)* Ch. Solitude Creek Sassy Fras, by Ch. Lyn-Mar Acres M'Lord Batuff ex Ch. Solitude Creek How Bout That, born July 1967. Bred and owned by Alice B. Lane. *(Bottom)* Ch. Solitude Creek Sycamore, by Ch. Lyn-Mar Acres M'Lord Batuff ex Ch. Solitude Creek How Bout That, born July 1967, handled by Bobby Barlow. Alice B. Lane, breeder-owner.

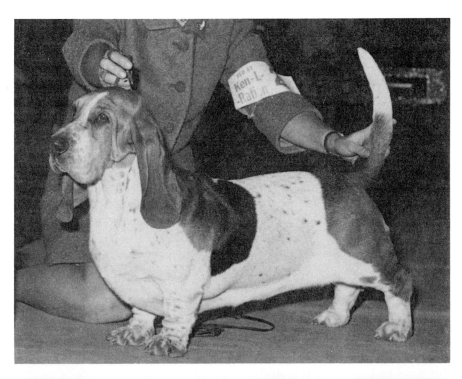

Stoneybluff

Stoneybluff Bassets had their beginning in 1965, following the loss of a much loved twelve-year-old Boxer dog who had been the pet of Frank J. and Virginia J. Kovalic at Milford, Michigan. The house seemed a very empty place after the Boxer's death, so the Kovalics, having read the announcements in the Detroit newspapers, visited the Detroit Kennel Club Dog Show and spent an entire day looking at various breeds, trying to decide what breed they would like to select for purchase. The Basset Hounds touched their hearts, and the excitement of the dog show caught their fancy. It was decided that a Basset would be their new breed and that they wanted a show dog.

The earliest attempts to start out in the dog show world were not too successful for these new fanciers. However, they were gaining knowledge, learning what is involved with breeding and showing. Their true introduction came about with the purchase of their foundation bitch, Champion Lyn Mar Acres Michelle, daughter of Champion Lyn Mar Acres Quick Trip and Champion Lyn Mar Acres M'Lord Batuff. At the same time a companion was purchased for "Missy," Champion Jagersven Monarch II, son of Champion Lyn Mar Acres Press Agent from Champion Jagersven Gigi.

For "Missy's" first litter, she was bred to Champion Lyn Mar Acres End Man, producing Champion Stoneybluff Ringer, who was Reserve Winners Dog at the 1973 Basset Hound Club of America Specialty. Ringer proved to be an important contributor to the future of Stoneybluff Kennels, siring Champions Stoneybluff Ferdinand and Lucky Charm, plus Stoneybluff Sherlock and Stoneybluff Nikoma.

For her second litter, "Missy" was bred to Champion Jagersven Monarch II and produced eight puppies. Five of that litter earned championships; Champion Stoneybluff Napoleon, who in turn sired Champions Stoneybluff Monarch and Contessa; Champion Stoneybluff Antoinette, who produced Stoneybluff Pocohontas; Champion Stoneybluff Desiree, who produced Champion Stoneybluff Abigail; and Champions Stoneybluff Caroline and Stoneybluff Jagersven Marie. "Missy" now has earned her place in the Register of Merit, sponsored by the Basset Hound Club of America honoring top producing sires and dams.

Through years of close linebreeding, the Kovalics have established a consistent type of animal characterized as the Stoneybluff Basset. They have bred to maintain the long, elegant dog with the refined

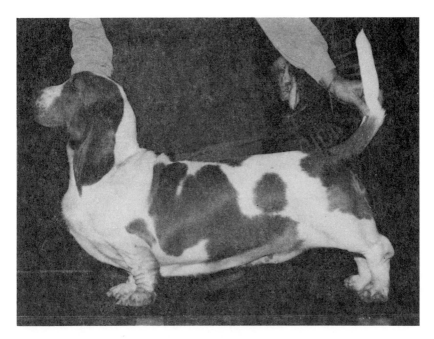

Ch. Stoneybluff Lady Jane, Winners Bitch at the Basset Hound Club of America Specialty, 1983. Bred and owned by Virginia and Frank Kovalic.

Ch. Stoneybluff Ringer, by Ch. Lyn Mar Acres End Man ex Ch. Lyn Mar Acres Michelle, taking Best of Winners at Macomb County Kennel Club when only two years old. Breeder-owners Virginia and Frank Kovalic.

head for which Lyn Mar Acres have been so well known and admired. They have put their time and energy into breeding and then showing the dogs to championship status. Their greatest satisfaction has been the number of Specialty wins achieved by the Stoneybluff line. Their latest campaigner as we go to press is Champion Stoneybluff Lady Jane, Winners Bitch at the 1983 Basset Hound Club of America Specialty held in Portland, Oregon.

Currently, Stoneybluff Oliver, the sire of Lady Jane and Champion Stoneybluff Prairie Flower (the latest bitch to gain championship honors) is continuing to make his contribution to the Basset world. Stoneybluff Cinnamon Stick and Stoneybluff Gertrude are now in the show ring, with each earning points toward their championships. Oliver's offspring from bitches outside of the Kovalics' own kennel are soon to make show debuts.

Ch. Lyn Mar Acres Michelle, the foundation bitch at Stoneybluff Bassets, bred by Mrs. Margaret S. Walton and owned by Frank J. Kovalic. Photo at one year of age.

Ch. Stoneybluff Napoleon taking Winners Dog at Associated Specialty Clubs of Chicago. Breeder-owners, Virginia and Frank Kovalic.

Champion Stoneybluff Monarch's sixteen-month-old daughter, Stoneybluff Tabatha, recently was awarded Reserve Winners Bitch at a Specialty, followed the next day with the same award from a breeder judge; and now she is making up points toward her title. Stoneybluff Teniel has been exported to England, owned there by Mrs. Mildred Seiffert of Maycombe Kennels. Teniel has just lately been released from quarantine and is being readied for England's show rings.

Stoneybluff Kennel usually carries 25 to 30 Bassets and over the years has achieved championship status on eighteen carrying the Stoneybluff name. With serious line-breeding, it is the Kovalics' intention and hope to continue maintaining a strong line of healthy, sound dogs consistent in type which can be readily identified as Stoneybluff hounds.

Strathalbyn

In St. Louis, Missouri, in December 1972, Mr. and Mrs. Eric George purchased their first ten Basset Hounds, the Bridlespur Pack. Since the early 1950's, the Bridlespurs had inbred their hounds, which originally came through the famous Greenly Hall Kennel (Fogleson) and Lyn Mar Acres Kennel (Walton). This pack had served as the loose basis for the other Midwest packs, namely Tantivy (Luce) and Strathalbyn (club-owned). Bridlespur had also produced the famous highest scoring obedience Basset of all time, Bridlespur Nudger (Taylor).

The Georges set about a very ambitious breeding program, based on the theory that twenty years of inbreeding had produced all the recessives, and things (hounds) were about as bad as they could get which was not really bad at all. Through English imports and from Lyn Mar Acres itself came new blood, but this new blood was carefully linebred from the original. The Georges did not appear on the competitive scene until October of 1973, at the National Pack Trials, where they won the Two Couple competition for field performance and bench merit. March 1974 saw them in the show ring for the first

Strathalbyn Bobbie, by Ch. Strathalbyn Scarface ex Lady Demand de Toma, taking Best of Winners for Mr. and Mrs. Eric George, Crescent, Missouri, at Southeast Missouri in June 1982.

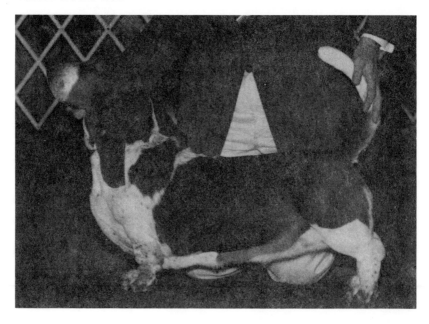

Ch. Strathalbyn Hit and Run finishing by going Best of Winners from the American-bred Class at Gateway Basset Hound Club 1980. Only twelve times in the ring as a special, this son of Ch. Strathalbyn Shoot To Kill, C.D., T.D. ex Lyn Mar Acres La Tache earned eleven Group placements. Owned by Mr. and Mrs. Eric George.

time. By August of that year, with their new blood infusion, they were placing in the Hound Group from the Puppy Classes.

The success of this large private kennel truly speaks for itself. Over 57 champions have been produced there, 43 of which have won at Group level. The Georges' Strathalbyn prefix is prominent in all the leading purebred packs, is very much in evidence in conformation competition, and has produced top obedience and tracking hounds as well.

Notable influential hounds from the Georges' Strathalbyns are American and Canadian Champion Strathalbyn Panic; Champion Strathalbyn Passport; Champion Strathalbyn Shoot To Kill, C.D., T.D.; Champion Strathalbyn Coldstream Eric; Champion Strathalbyn Hit and Run; Champion Strathalbyn War Paint; Champion Strathalbyn War Lord; Champion Strathalbyn Skylarking; Champion Strathalbyn Sorceress; Champion Strathalbyn Legacy; and the outstanding young bitch Strathalbyn Reliance, from whom the Georges expect the foundation for their next ten years of breeding.

Tal-E-Ho

Tal-E-Ho Bassets, owned by Henry and Ann Jerman at West Islip, New York, are widely known and highly respected producers of top quality, with dogs from this kennel or sired by the dogs from there gaining many honors.

The list of Tal-E-Ho champions is a long one, but pride of place among them goes to American and Canadian Champion Tal-E-Ho's Prancer, born in 1970, who started his career at eight months, completing his championship two months later from the bred-by-Exhibitor Class. At fourteen months of age, Prancer won the Basset Hound Club of America National Specialty. He eventually set a record of twelve Specialty wins.

Himself the sire of 40 American Champions (and the grandsire of many more), Prancer was by Tal-E-Ho's George ex Tal-E-Ho's Ka Ro. Among his best known sons was American and Canadian Champion Tal-E-Ho Top Banana (from Tal-E-Ho's Dorinda)—a dog who was widely admired and who accomplished great things for the Martins at Northwoods Kennels.

These two four-week old baby Bassets are typical of the quality that has made Tal-E-Ho so famous and successful a kennel over the years. Henry and Ann Jerman, owners.

Timber Ridge's Strathalbyn Lord Snuggley, by Ch. Strathalbyn War Paint ex Ch. Strathalbyn Lilley, photographed in 1983 at Timber Ridge. Meena Rogers, owner.

Timber Ridge

The Timber Ridge Bassets, organized in 1946 and recognized in 1947 by the National Beagle Club, was the first recognized pack of Basset hounds in the United States. It is the fourth oldest, continuous, recognized, active pack of foot hounds in this country today. The three older packs of foot hounds are the Sir Sister Beagles, in Massachusetts; the Wolver Beagles, in Virginia; and Nantucket-Treweryn Beagles, in Massachusetts and Virginia, recognized in 1903, 1913, and 1924 respectively. The Timber Ridge Bassets were founded by Charles R. and Amelia F. Rogers, who serve as Master and Huntsman, respectively.

Timber Ridge is a private pack, supported by subscription, which hunts approximately ten couples of tricolored, purebred A.K.C.-registered Bassets.

Amelia Rogers hunts cottontail rabbit in various counties of Maryland and also hunts in Pennsylvania and Virginia by invitation.

The pack hunts Sunday afternoons from October to April and two or three times a week. The hunt takes about two hours over rolling country, which covers agricultural areas, grassland, wooded areas, and much heavy underbrush (honeysuckle, multiflora, and so on).

Timber Ridge has an average field of 85 subscribers of all ages, from babies carried papoose-style to those in their mid-eighties.

The original hunting stock came from the early private packs of Gerald Livingston's Kilsyth, on Long Island, New York; Mrs. Consuelo Ford's Bijoux, on the Eastern Shore of Maryland; and Betty Porter's Upland Kennels, in Pennsylvania. Unfortunately, that great old breeding is in the dim background of today's Bassets' pedigrees.

Since then Timber Ridge has tried bloodlines from most of the serious breeders of Bassets in this country: Peg Walton's Lyn Mar, Ira Shoop's Hartshead, Leslie Kelly's Belbay, hounds from Tulpehocken, the Bucher's Warwick Kennels, from Norwood and Mildred Engle, Chris Teeter's Long View Acres, Ola DeGroat's De-Alo, Eve and Joe McKenna's Coldstream, Jane Luce's Tantivy, Don LaRue's Blue Lick, and Eric and Erica George's Strathalbyn.

Hounds in the Rogers pack are big (they average 65 pounds) and must be of a rangy-type for this country: strong, sound, agile, and built to stay—something like a fine race horse. They must be broad between the point of shoulders but fairly narrow between the front legs, their loin and hind legs well sprung. They cannot be built like a sprinter, *i.e.*, like a quarter horse, short-coupled, a lot of daylight between their front legs.

There is much discussion about the ideal Basset type. Many show people want straight front legs, therefore set well out, body very low to the ground; the weight is suspended. Having hunted a pack of Bassets for 30-odd years, Amelia Rogers decidedly prefers a half-crook, the chest cupped in the crook with front legs well under the chest for support. The massive weight is then supported by the legs instead of being suspended between the two. Bassets whose weights are suspended "will break down in the hunting field, having no spring to take up the shock and weight," according to Mrs. Rogers; and, she goes on to state, "as Bassets are hunters, I feel it is a very undesirable quality."

At Timber Ridge Kennels eight or more hounds are kenneled together in each of two large grass runs. These enclose a hillside and stream and total about three and a half acres. Their houses are tight, draft-proof, and unheated; and they are built in a continuous U-shaped compound facing south with east and west wings. The compound is one-room deep, with many single rooms and some rooms holding four or more if they wish, thus allowing each hound a choice of sleeping accommodations. The dogs may lie on the roofs in the sun or on decks in front of the houses. In summer there is plenty of shade, and sections of

Timber Ridge Basset entry at Bryn Mawr Hound Show 1955, Engle's Speedy Ace. 1st in Entered Dog, 2nd in Stallion Hound, 1st Couple of Dog Hounds (with Upland Bosco), and Champion Basset dog at this event. Charles R. Rogers, M B H, handler.

Timber Ridge Bassets at the Bryn Mawr Hound Show 1960, where they won Best Five Couple Pack. Charles R. Rogers, Master. Meena Rogers, Whipper-In. Mrs. Alfred Bissell (Stockford Bassets), judge. At center front is Win Dee Hill Hedge Hopper, by Ch. Warwick So Great ex Warwick Fidelia (granddaughter of Ch. Lyn Mar Acres Clown).

Champion Basset Bitch, Timber Ridge Mellow, by Ch. Meyer's Red Boy Smith's Jezebel, Meena Rogers handling at Bryn Mawr Hound Show 1957.

the houses open for air circulation. There are three small grass runs with houses holding two to four hounds. Three gravel runs for emergencies, bitches in heat, or whatever are in a separate bank barn. Mrs. Rogers has found that hounds stay much fitter in these large grass runs, running down the hillside and back to bark at any sign of wildlife, but the main advantage of this open space is to allow them to play and roughhouse. They make up games of tag regularly three or four times a day, with first one and then another being "it." It is interesting how universal this game is. It seems to be a combination of inventiveness, agility, war, affection, and mastering difficult maneuvers and obstacles—great fun!

Timber Ridge uses a dry kibble as food for the dogs. The kibble is dispensed in a self-feeding system in hog-feeders holding up to one hundred pounds at a time. There is water at all times, mainly from automatic, heated troughs, although the grass runs cross a stream. Incidentally, the hounds enjoy this watering spot very much, wading and lying down in it to cool off on a hot summer day. Even in the dead of winter, with heavy snow on the ground, their well-worn paths wander down to the stream and across to the trees and cover on the opposite bank.

To describe the Timber Ridge Bassets hunting as a pack, we quote Mrs. Rogers:

> Hounds are taken out of the kennels as a pack (*i.e.,* collected). Allowed to empty and settle down, then walked to a given point, given a signal on the English hunting horn and encouraged by voice to go into cover. They all scatter and fan out searching for game. One hound might suddenly get very animated, stern feathering madly, others will notice and join in the search. Soon up pops a rabbit and she's gone away. Outlying hounds will hark to the others and all will be on in hot pursuit, giving tongue with their extraordinary voices. We pursue this rabbit, or line, as long as possible until they put her to ground or lose the scent. Then off in search of another, over crop land, up and down hills, woods, over and through streams, dense bramble, honeysuckle and lush pasture. All the while as a unit (pack). After about two hours, we call them in, pack up and call it a day. When they get back to the kennels or in the van driving home, they settle down to the serious job of grooming each other, seeing that all are dry and clean, all very tired and contented.

Topohil

Topohil Bassets at Mars Hill, N. Carolina, came about *despite* the first Basset owned by Mrs. Jean L. Sheehy and her family. This dog was named Caleb and came from the dog pound. It did not take the Sheehys long to discover *why* he had been in the pound. To quote Jean:

> The first thing he did was to knock down and scratch one of the neighbor's children. He would get up on my bed and refuse to let me in it. He would eat anything that wasn't nailed down, including a Christmas corsage that my mother had pinned on her coat—ornaments and all. If you opened a door, he was long gone. When he died during an operation, I firmly stated *no more dogs* in general, and Basset Hounds in particular.

This resolution lasted about two weeks, during which time Jean's husband and daughter spent all their waking hours trying to convince her that they must have another Basset. Eventually she succumbed to their pleading, and Woodville's Forester (by Woodville's Chorus ex Woodville's Frolic), whelped on January 24th 1963, bred by Harriet C. Smyth, was purchased. This occurred only after Curt Sheehy had agreed to take the puppy to obedience classes. "Benny" never did get an obedience degree, for in typical Basset fashion he was the ultimate clown and would think of things to do along the way to get laughs, which he did. However, while still going through his three Beginner (a record which Jean believes he still holds to this day) and two Pre-Novice Classes, people kept looking admiringly at him and asking Jean if she planned to show him. Jean was not even quite sure then what a dog show might be, but she was talked into going to a match show; and when Benny won the breed and placed in the group, she was ecstatic. Point shows followed; and Benny, owner-handled, accumulated all but one major toward his championship, all at shows within a 50-mile radius of the Sheehys' home. Why they stopped showing him before he finished, Mrs. Sheehy adds, is "another long story."

The following year the Sheehys purchased Mischievous Molly from Mrs. Frances Scaife. Molly was born in July 1964 and was a daughter of Champion The Ring's Ali Baba ex Hubertus Dolly Madison. Molly gained her Companion Dog degree and then made a career for herself doing commercial advertisements. This job came about by her having been the only Basset entered at the Westchester Kennel Club Dog

Ch. Topohil's Glory Bea and puppies belonging to Jean Sheehy, Topohil Bassets, Georgetown, Connecticut.

Ch. Topohil Owenna owned by Mrs. Jean Sheehy, Topohil Bassets.

Show in obedience one year when one of the animal talent agencies needed a Basset for an ad; the agent telephoned to see if Molly would be available. She was.

Molly was bred to Woodville's Forester and produced a litter during May 1967. The Sheehys kept two puppies from this litter: Topohil's Andrea, who also achieved her obedience degree; and Topohil's Gros Chien Rouge, whose claim to fame was that she was Curt Sheehy's constant companion until her death at thirteen and a half years of age. Molly's second litter, by Champion Galway's Meshak, produced only one puppy, the Sheehys' Topohil Cotton Candy, born in May 1968.

Ch. Windamohr Autumn of Topohil taking Best of Winners and Best of Opposite Sex at the Basset Hound Club of Long Island Specialty. Owned by Mrs. Jean L. Sheehy.

Candy gained her C.D. degree and also did many advertisements and commercials. She produced one litter and then had to be spayed. This litter, sired by Champion Forestbay Montgomery, gave the Sheehys their Champion Topohil's Glory Bea and Champion Topohil's Gypsy, born Mary 1972. Both Glory Bea and Gypsy had wins at Specialty shows and had Group placements; and when Glory was bred to her half-brother, Champion Manor Hill Father James, she produced the Sheehys' Champion Topohill Ovation and Champion Topohil Owenna.

In early 1968, the Sheehys purchased Abbot Run Valley Gayle (Abbot Run Valley Gabby ex Champion Abbot Run Valley Brass Beauty), born November 1967 and bred by Marjorie Brandt and Joseph Roan. Gayle was bred to Champion Yclept Bruiser, producing Champion Topohil's Kathy's Honey and Braz, and Champion Topohil's Idoneous. When bred to Champion Forestbay Montgomery she produced Champion Topohil Leader of the Pack (who now also has champion get) and Champion Topohil Low and Behold.

In 1970 the Sheehys obtained Double B's Lord Chesterfield and Forestbay Montgomery, and they decided to show seriously in breed competition. Prior to this time, after "Benny," they had entered sporadically in breed, mostly to support local Specialties; they much preferred obedience.

Champion Double B's Lord Chesterfield (Champion Double B's B.M.O.C. ex Champion Double B's Final Fling) was born in 1969 and bred by Helen P. Boutell. Co-ownership on him was given by the Sheehys to their dear friend Beatrice Connolly, and upon completion of his championship he went to live with her, where he is thoroughly spoiled and still enjoying life.

Champion Forestbay Montgomery (Champion Forestbay Joshua ex Forestbay Manor Hill Mahalia), born in 1969, was bred by Forestbay Kennels. He finished title easily, was a multiple Specialty winner, and ranked as one of the Top Ten Bassets three years consecutively although he was never extensively campaigned. Despite the fact that he was used only 26 times at stud during his lifetime, Montgomery's champion get have proven the adage "quality begets quality." Montgomery passed away on June 18th 1980, but his legacy will be with us for years to come. Among his progeny are Champion Manor Hill Tooth Fairy, Champion Manor Hill Father James, and Champion Manor Hill Molly Molly, bred by Joan Scholz; Champion Topohil's Glory Bea and Champion Topohil's Gypsy, bred by Jean Sheehy; Champion Riverlane Musher Diane, bred by Howard and Blackie Nygood; Champion Topohil's Blossom Seeley, bred by Arthur and Susan Vinson; Champion Topohil's Leader of the Pack and Champion Topohil Low and Behold, bred by Jean Sheehy; Champion Len-Jo's Traces of Love, bred by Allen and Mackie Githens; Champion Bar-Wick's Shortstop, bred by Barbara Wicklund; Champion Manor Hill Mayday, bred by Joan Scholz; Champion Topohil Tailor Made, bred by Jean Sheehy; and Brazilian Champion Topohil's Here's Hermione, bred by Dorothy Willis and Jean Sheehy.

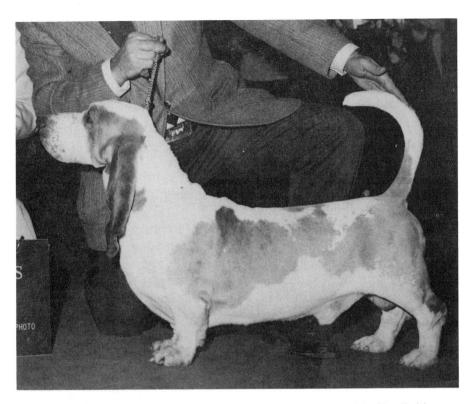

Ch. Topohil Leader of the Pack taking points en route to the title. Handled by Howard Nygood for Mrs. Jean L. Sheehy, Georgetown, Connecticut.

The Sheehys have always kept their kennel small, so that each dog can receive individual attention. Their kennel building is 12″ by 24′ and has six individual runs off each side. It has a large "puppy room" with a run off that; however, Jean comments that "puppies have lived in it only once to my recollection. It is now generally used to house bitches in season." The puppies are whelped in the house and any that the Sheehys keep remain there until they are at least six months old. The oldest dog is also given permanent house residence, the others rotating into the house for one week at a time. In addition to the kennel runs, there is a large paddock area (50′ by 100′) for daily exercise.

Residents at Topohil as we write are Champion Forestbay Leader of the Pack, Champion Windamohr Autumn of Topohil, Champion Topohil Owenna, Champion Topohil Ovation, Champion Topohil Tailor Made, and Champion Topohil Connecticut Yankee.

Windmaker

It was early in the 1960's when James R. and Wanda A. White started with Basset Hounds as owners of the breed, but it was not until about 1965 that they began taking an interest in breeding and showing them. In 1975 their kennel name, "Windmaker," was registered with the American Kennel Club and since then the majority of their dogs have been given "weather" names.

The breeding program really started to line up with the purchase of Santana-Mandeville Gwendy, but unfortunately she died shortly after the Whites acquired her. Next Keithann Rag Doll was purchased with far happier results as she became the Top Producing Basset Bitch of 1973. She was a daughter of Champion Santana-Mandeville Rodney (Champion Santana-Mandeville Tarzan ex Champion Gwendolyn of Mandeville) from Champion Hubertus Diamond Li'l (Champion Lime Tree Micawber ex Champion Hubertus Lazy Betty). Brigadier's Swamp Fox, strong in Lyn Mar Acres breeding, was the Whites' foundation stud, to whom Rag Doll was bred and by whom she produced the Whites' first two homebred champions, Champion Keithann Wendy and Champion Windmaker's Summer Storm.

Bred to Champion Lyn Mar Acres M'Lord Batuff, Summer Storm produced Champion Windmaker's Storm Warning, Champion Windmaker's Southern Storm, Windmaker's Summer Breeze, and Windmaker's Black Storm. Storm Warning was Best of Opposite Sex at the Basset Hound Club of America National Specialty in 1974. Black Storm died of cancer shortly after earning her C.D. degree and winning Best of Breed and a third in Group from the classes in one day. She belonged to Shirley Hiatt.

In 1976 the Whites obtained Windmaker's Sadiron Connie from Nell and Jerry Looper. They had sent the Loopers a bitch, Champion Windmaker's Indian Summer, a couple of years earlier, the arrangement being that the Whites would receive a puppy in return later on. Connie was (and still is) a beautiful bitch. After completing her championship she was bred to Champion Lochopt Halcyon Collegian; the resulting litter included Champion Windmaker's Hurricane Jody, Champion Windmaker's Man Of All Seasons, Champion Windmaker's Summer Thunder, and Windmaker's Sadiron Dixie. The latter died of parvovirus shortly after winning a five-point major at a Basset Specialty from the Puppy Class. Both males have Group

Ch. Windmaker's Man of All Seasons. Born March 1979, littermate to Ch. Windmaker's Summer Thunder and Ch. Hurricane Jody, bred, owned and handled by James R. and Wanda A. White.

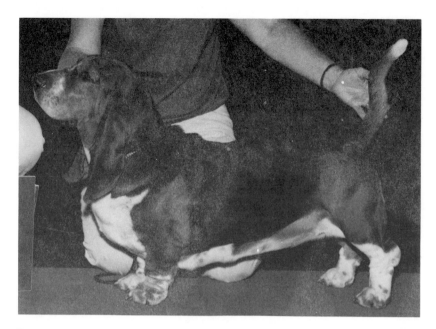

This dam of six champions, Ch. Windmaker's Sadiron Connie, ROM, is by Ch. Coran's My Pick o'George ex Ch. Windmaker's Indian Summer. Bred by Nell and Jerry Cooper and owned by James R. and Wanda White.

Windmaker's Black Storm, littermate to Champions Windmaker's Southern Storm, Storm Warning and Summer Breeze, sadly died needing just one major to complete title. Bred and owned by James R. and Wanda A. White.

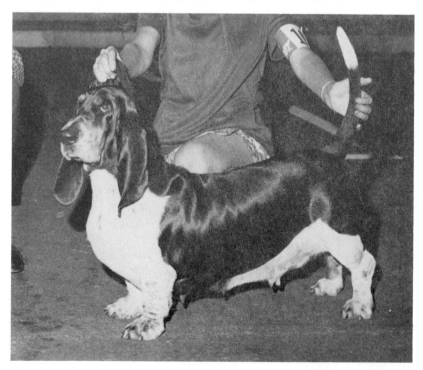

Ch. Windmaker's Storm Warning taking Best of Opposite Sex at the Basset Hound Club of America Specialty in 1974. Owned by James and Wanda White, Jim White handling.

placements although shown sparingly. Champion Windmaker's Bermuda High and Champion Windmaker's Lochopt Connex were from a breeding of Connie to the Cromleys' Champion Ran Su Lochopt J.D. This was a lovely litter and the Cromleys did quite well with their bitch from it.

Bermuda High died three weeks in whelp to Summer Thunder, a litter over which the Whites had been much excited in anticipation but which was not to be.

Recently the Whites have made the decision to do no more breeding since Jim is becoming increasingly busy and popular as a judge. Currently they are showing a young Fox Terrier bitch whom they bred. Wanda comments, "This is a whole new ball game, but I have always liked terriers so three years ago we bought a smooth bitch from Madison Weeks, finished her, then tried our hand at breeding them."

Aust. Ch. Sagaces Merryman, born July 1981, is a multi-Best in Show winner with impressive wins under local and overseas judges. He has recently gained the highest win ever accorded a Basset in Australia—Best in Show at the prestigious Sydney Royal Easter Show. Bred and owned by Sue and Barry Millar, Sydney, Australia.

Chapter 5

Bassets in Australia

The charms of the Basset Hound have in no way been overlooked by Australian fanciers, and we are pleased to note and bring you photos of some very high-quality dogs who were bred there.

At the top of the list is Australian Champion Sagaces Merryman, who achieved the notable honor of taking best in Show at Australia's most prestigious event, the Sydney Royal Easter Show. This was in addition to other Best in Show wins during his career, some Reserve Best Exhibit in Show awards, and multiple Best Hound Exhibit victories. The Sydney Royal, owing to its size and quality, is conceded to be a show of very special importance, thus the winning of Best in Show there is a particularly coveted honor, and it is the most important win achieved to date by an Australian Basset.

Merryman is not only himself a homebred, but his dam is also. She is Australian Champion Sagaces Harmony, who was whelped in January 1977, a daughter of Australian Champion Hushanda Ezaruffyn Too ex Australian Champion Kelcliffe Candida. Harmony had an impressive list of wins to her credit as a show bitch, and she has certainly contributed tremendously to her breed as a producer. A littermate to Merryman, Australian Champion Sagaces Major Dundee, although somewhat overshadowed by Merryman's successes, is doing some splendid winning as well with numerous Best Hound Exhibit and Reserve Best in Show awards to his credit.

Sue and Barry Millar are presently watching with interest and anticipation the progress of a young litter at their kennel by Australian Champion Hushanda Kid Gloves from Harmony. All of these youngsters are red and white and all look to be of truly excellent type.

Sagaces Casper, another from the "C" litter by Aust. Ch. Hushanda Kid Gloves ex Aust. Ch. Sagaces Harmony. Sue and Barry Millar, owners.

Sagaces Conroy, by Aust. Ch. Hushanda Kid Gloves ex Aust. Ch. Sagace's Harmony, bred and owned by Sue and Barry Millar. Littermates to Sagaces Charity, Clarrie, Casper and Corker.

Sagaces Charity, by Aust. Ch. Hushanda Kid Gloves ex Aust. Ch. Sagaces Harmony, littermate to Sagaces Clarrie, Casper, Corker and Conroy. Bred and owned by Sue and Barry Millar.

This lovely bitch is Australian Ch. Sagaces Harmony, born January 1977, bred and owned by Sue and Barry Millar. A daughter of Aust. Ch. Hushanda Ezaruffyn Too ex Aust. Ch. Kelcliffe Candida, she was highly successful in the show ring before retirement to produce some very outstanding offspring.

Sagaces Clarrie is another handsome member of the litter which includes Sagaces Charity, Casper Corker and Conroy. Homebreds owned by Sue and Barry Millar.

Looking back into history, Bassets first appeared in Australia during 1893. Word of the breed had been brought there by Sir Everett Millais, referred to so extensively in our British historical chapter, who had journeyed to Australia during the 1880's for reasons of health. Sir Everett, I am sure, never lost the opportunity of extolling the virtues of his beloved breed, the Basset, and I am certain that he left the Australian fanciers extremely anxious to become personally acquainted with these dogs.

118

The first Basset to arrive in Australia was Levity, who came there to Mrs. Anderson and Mrs. McLoughlin.

It was not until 1957 that any real Basset activity got underway among Australian fanciers. Then a dog and two bitches in whelp were imported, the dog unnamed so far as I can find, but the bitches were Brockleton Country Maid and Grim's Caroline.

It is interesting that the fanciers who were most involved with early Australian Bassets were the now world-famous judge Dr. Harold Spira of Sydney and John Mackinolty.

Dr. Spira's Chevalier Kennels became very widely known, and progeny from his dogs did much to popularize Bassets throughout Australia. His imports from Great Britain included Champion Grim's Vanquish, Fochno Chestnut, and Sykemoor Dauphin.

Currently showing Bassets in Australia, in addition to the Millars, one finds Mrs. J. Beckman with Champion Cathjaa Careworn Sir (by Australian Champion Basjambe The Dependable ex Cathjaa Ablaze), born in 1979, and some puppies by this dog winning well. S.C. McHenry and Mrs. E.C. McHenry have Champion Hushanda Harvester, born in 1978, by Australian Champion Hushanda Ezaruffyn Too ex Australian Champion Hushanda Mrs. Miranda; and Champion Hushanda Trailblazer, born in 1980, by Australian Champion Hushanda Burnt Embers ex Australian Champion Hushanda Im Trouble Too. V.E. and Mrs. M.J. Tinsley have Australian Champion Wahabi Wiseman and Australian Champion Houndsley Trendy Gal, and Mrs. R. Tissington has Australian Champion Jimetta Misty Morn. These are just some of the interested breeders actively participating in the Basset Fancy in Australia.

Zizanie's Rasputin taking Best of Winners at the Metropolitan Kennel Club in Canada in 1976.

Chapter 6

Basset Hounds in Canada

The Basset Hound Club of Canada was founded in 1959 and held its first Specialty Show the following year. During the 1960's the breed made great strides in popularity in Canada; and as judges who officiate frequently at Canadian shows, the authors can attest that we have found quality to be high and competition interesting during the past decade.

The earliest Bassets known in Canada were three listed as entries at a dog show in 1903. Both smooth and rough-coated Bassets were on record as "officially recognized breeds" in Canada during the first decade of the present century. The first Basset registered by the Canadian Kennel Club was Al's Janet, owned by N.E. Pegg, in 1936.

Canadian breeders over the years have imported some of the leading bloodlines from the United States, including Greenly Hall, Lyn Mar Acres, Notrenom, Santana-Mandeville, Hartshead, and many more. Basset interest exists in all sections of Canada.

We are pleased to bring you photos of some of the Canadian winners, along with kennel stories to give our readers some idea of what is taking place in Basset circles in Canada.

Chantinghall

Chantinghall Basset Hounds at Wainfleet, Ontario, Canada, were founded in 1959 by Mrs. Rosemary McKnight who is a well-known judge in addition to being a highly successful Basset breeder.

Mrs. McKnight's dogs include some very special and important winners. One example is the exquisite bitch Canadian and American Champion Chantinghall Aire 'n Graces, whose show record includes the remarkable accomplishment of having been Top Basset Bitch in Canada for 1975, 1976, and 1977 and Top Hound in Canada for 1975 and 1976. A daughter of Canadian and American Champion Chantinghall's Dominic ex Canadian and American Champion Eve-Ning's Over the Rainbow, "Gracie" is a homebred.

Can. and Am. Ch. Chantinghall Nan Tucket, by Can. and Am. Ch. Chantinghall Dominic ex Can. Ch. Chantinghall Cousin Maud, was bred by Rosemary McKnight and is owned by Linda and Peter Weaver in Canada.

Can. and Am. Ch. Chantinghall Aire 'n Graces II, by Can. and Am. Ch. Chantinghall Dominic ex Can. and Am. Ch. Eve-Ning's Over the Rainbow. "Gracie" was Top Basset Bitch in all of Canada in 1975, 1976, 1977, and No. 8 Hound in 1975 and 1976. Breeder-owner, Rosemary McKnight.

Canadian and American Champion Chantinghall Blockbuster, by Canadian and American Champion Chantinghall Dominic ex Chantinghall Mary Kate, was the Top Winning Basset Male in all of Canada for 1980. Bred by Liz Lors, he, too, belongs to Rosemary McKnight.

The sire of both of these record-holding Bassets is himself a most distinguished dog, Canadian and American Champion Chantinghall Dominic. A son of Canadian and American Champion Solitude Creek Sophocles ex Canadian Champion Chantinghall Amethyst, he, also, is a homebred owned by Rosemary McKnight. Dominic is the sire of eighteen champions to date. His dam is litter-sister to English Champion Chantinghall Ancestor.

Another very excellent Dominic daughter (from Canadian Champion Chantinghall Cousin Maud) is Canadian and American Champion Chantinghall Nan Tucket, who made a fine record in the United States as well as in Canada during the late 1970's.

Mrs. McKnight has become a very popular judge whose services are constantly in demand.

Am. and Can. Ch. Beaujangles Jackson Brown, by Bar-B Buckets O'Sullivan ex Belyn's Jezebel of Beaujangles owned by Ivan W. and Mrs. Phyllis Macklin.

Fiveacres

Fiveacres Bassets, at Winnipeg, Manitoba, in Canada, are owned by Ivan W. Macklin and Mrs. Phyllis Macklin, who formerly bred Bassets under the prefix "Parkside."

Among the foundation stock here one finds American and Canadian Champion Harper's Bart of Parkside, who was purchased from Medora Harper in Omaha, Nebraska, in October 1972, just in time to make the entry closing for the November show at Regina in Saskatchewan. That weekend resulted in championship honors for Bart, plus two Hound Group firsts. Since he was still a gangly puppy even though a champion, it was decided to shelve him for awhile to grow up before entering competition as a Special.

During 1973 and 1974, Bart was shown in the United States along with his half-brother Parkside's Darby O'Gill. Both gained their American titles plus helping their sire, Champion Harper's Rhett Butler, to become Top Producing Stud Dog for 1974.

Bart had one trip to Bermuda during which he picked up several points there, but he never did return to finish.

By 1975 it was felt that he was ready to enter Specials in Canada, and in that year he won a Best in Show. Of course, his career then continued, and owner-handled he was shown everywhere that weekend travel would permit. He became Top Basset in Canada that year and

Am. and Can. Ch. Parkside's Indian Emperor, by Harper's Rhett Butler ex Island Park's Fickle Fran, with his American friend and handler Jack Potts winning one of two 5-point majors gained in   Texas. Bred and owned by Ivan W. Macklin and Mrs. Phyllis M. Macklin.

additionally was Number Seven Hound. He was shown sparingly after that and, to quote Mrs. Macklin, "used as a stud dog when we could get him down off the couch."

Bart was a grandson of Champion Orangepark Dexter and Champion Musicland's Casey Jones.

American, Canadian, and Bermudian Champion Parkside's Darby O'Gill was also a son of Champion Harper's Rhett Butler but he was the product of a Canadian-bred female, Island Park Fickle Fran, from Mrs. W. Stevenson's kennel, Portage La Prairie, well known for quality Bassets.

Darby's first show early in 1973 resulted in two Best Hound Puppy awards, and he finished quickly. As already mentioned, he and Bart fought it out for the majors in the United States during 1973 and 1974, Darby finishing more quickly than Bart with Group placings from the classes.

When Bart retired in 1976, Darby became Canada's Number One Basset for that year. Then in early 1977 he made his last trip to Bermuda to finish. When he returned home it was found he had glandular cancer, from which he had, unknown to his owners, been suffering for quite awhile. He died just before his fifth birthday in late May. His loss was keenly felt for many years to follow. Again quoting Mrs. Macklin, "He was a dog who never, ever let you down."

In 1977, American and Canadian Champion Parkside's Indian Emperor tried to follow in his brother's footsteps, but it wasn't for him. He had the quality but not the "weekend stuff" it takes to spend a full year on the road. So in August he came home with many trophies and ribbons to be the "cop" in the kennel, ordering everyone around and keeping everything under control. Mrs. Macklin was too busy to find the majors in the United States, so "Joe," as Indian Emperor was called, went to his Texas friend Jack Potts who picked up two five-point majors in one weekend with him in that state.

"Joe" now spends his time in the living room enjoying the life of a family dog.

Canadian Champion Parkside's Nikkson, C.D., by Champion Island Park's Nikki ex Champion Harper's Rhonda; Champion Fiveacres Joyelle, by Parkside's M. and M. ex Beartooth Freda; and Champion Half and Half Fiveacres, by Fiveacres Special Blend ex Pott's Lady of Cara are other champions associated with this kennel. Beartooth Freda, by Champion Beartooth Norman ex Beartooth Kitty, is also a fine Basset from Fiveacres.

Ch. Zizanie's Halloween Snoopy, well-known Canadian winner of the late 1970's.

Ch. Glenborne Mighty Bruiser, by Fiveacres Special Blend ex Beartooth Beth, owned by Ivan W. and Mrs. Phyllis Macklin.

Chapter 7

Standards of the Breed

The standard of the breed, to which one sees and hears such frequent reference whenever purebred dogs are written of or discussed, is the word picture of what is considered to be the ideal specimen of the breed in question. It outlines, in minute detail, each and every feature of this breed, both in physical characteristics and in temperament, accurately describing the dog from whisker to tail, creating a clear impression of what is to be considered correct or incorrect, the features comprising "breed type," and the probable temperament and behavior pattern of typical members of that breed.

The standard is the guide for breeders endeavoring to produce quality dogs and for fanciers wishing to learn what is considered beautiful in the breed, and it is the tool with which judges evaluate and make their decisions in the ring. The dog it describes is the one which we seek and to which we compare in making our evaluations. It is the result of endless hours spent in dedicated work by knowledgeable members of each parent Specialty club, resulting from the combined efforts of the club itself, its individual members, and finally the American Kennel Club by whom official approval must be granted prior to each standard's acceptance, or that of any amendments or changes to it, in the United States. In Great Britain, the governing body for all purebred dogs is the Kennel Club. Breed standards are based on intensive study of breed history, earlier standards in the United States, and the purposes for which the breed was originally created and developed. All such factors have played their part in the drawing up of our present standards.

128

These Bassets adorned an English post card which went through the mail in 1935. From a painting by Arthur Wardle.

Vernon Stokes's famous "Basset Hounds Hunting," from the author's collection of Hound memorabilia.

American Standard

GENERAL APPEARANCE: The Basset Hound possesses in marked degree those characteristics which equip it admirably to follow a trail over and through difficult terrain. It is a short-legged dog, heavier in bone, size considered, than any other breed of dog, and while its movement is deliberate, it is in no sense clumsy. In temperament it is mild, never sharp or timid. It is capable of great endurance in the field and is extreme in its devotion.

HEAD   The head is large and well proportioned, its length from occiput to muzzle is greater than the width at the brow. In over-all appearance the head is of medium width. *The skull* is well domed, showing a pronounced occipital protuberance. A broad flat skull is a fault. The length from nose to stop is approximately the length from stop to occiput. The sides are flat and free from cheek bumps. Viewed in profile the top lines of the muzzle and skull are straight and lie in parallel planes, with a moderately defined stop. The skin over the whole of the head is loose, falling in distinct wrinkles over the brow when the head is lowered. A dry head and tight skin are faults. *The muzzle* is deep, heavy, and free from snipiness. *The nose* is darkly pigmented, preferably black, with large wide-open nostrils. A deep liver-colored nose conforming to the coloring of the head is permissible but not desirable. *The teeth* are large, sound, and regular, meeting in either a scissors or an even bite. A bite either overshot or undershot is a serious fault. *The lips* are darkly pigmented and are pendulous, falling squarely in front and, toward the back, in loose hanging flews. *The dewlap* is very pronounced. *The neck* is powerful, of good length, and well arched. *The eyes* are soft, sad, and slightly sunken, showing a prominent haw, and in color are brown, dark brown preferred. A somewhat lighter-colored eye conforming to the general coloring of the dog is acceptable but not desirable. Very light or protruding eyes are faults. *The ears* are extremely long, low set, and when drawn forward, fold well over the end of the nose. They are velvety in texture, hanging in loose folds with the ends curling slightly inward. They are set far back on the head at the base of the skull and, in repose, appear to be set on the neck. A high set or flat ear is a serious fault.

FOREQUARTERS: *The chest* is deep and full with prominent sternum showing clearly in front of the legs. *The shoulders* and elbows are set close against the sides of the chest. The distance from the deepest

Ch. Abbot Run Valley Brassy, by Ch. Lyn-Mar Acres Top Brass ex Ch. Ro-Fre La Reine de la Balle, had a most successful career in two years' time. This outstanding red and white male is owned by Roger Fedette and Walter F. Brandt, Cumberland, Rhode Island.

point of the chest to the ground, while it must be adequate to allow free movement when working in the field, is not to be more than one-third the total height at the withers of an adult Basset. The shoulders are well laid back and powerful. Steepness in shoulder, fiddle fronts, and elbows that are out are serious faults. *The forelegs* are short, powerful, heavy in bone, with wrinkled skin. Knuckling over of the front legs is a disqualification. *The paw* is massive, very heavy with tough heavy pads, well rounded and with both feet inclined equally a trifle outward, balancing the width of the shoulders. Feet down at the pastern are serious fault. *The toes* are neither pinched together nor splayed, with the weight of the forepart of the body borne evenly on each. The dewclaws may be removed.

Overleaf: →

Ch. Manor Hill Mayday, by Ch. Forestbay Montgomery ex Manor Hill Free Spirit, bred by Joan Scholz and owned by Jean Sheehy. Winner Best of Breed, handled here by Howard Nygood.

BODY: The rib structure is long, smooth, and extends well back. The ribs are well sprung, allowing adequate room for heart and lungs. Flatsidedness and flanged ribs are faults. The topline is straight, level, and free from any tendency to sag or roach, which are faults.

HINDQUARTERS: The hindquarters are very full and well rounded, and are approximately equal to the shoulders in width. They must not appear slack or light in relation to the over-all depth of the body. The dog stands firmly on its hind legs showing a well-let-down stifle with no tendency toward a crouching stance. Viewed from behind, the hind legs are parallel, with the hocks turning neither in nor out. Cowhocks or bowed legs are serious faults. The hind feet point straight ahead. Steep, poorly angulated hindquarters are a serious fault. The dew-claws, if any, may be removed.

TAIL: The tail is not to be docked, and is set in continuation of the spine with but slight curvature, and carried gaily in hound fashion. The hair on the underside of the tail is coarse.

SIZE: The height should not exceed 14 inches. Height over 15 inches at the highest point of the shoulder blades is a disqualification.

GAIT: The Basset Hound moves in a smooth, powerful, and effortless manner. Being a scenting dog with short legs, it holds its nose low to the ground. Its gait is absolutely true with perfect co-ordination between the front and hind legs, and it moves in a straight line with hind feet following in line with the front feet, the hocks well bent with no stiffness of action. The front legs do not paddle, weave, or overlap, and the elbows must lie close to the body. Going away, the hind legs are parallel.

COAT: The coat is hard, smooth, and short, with sufficient density to be of use in all weather. The skin is loose and elastic. A distinctly long coat is a disqualification.

COLOR: Any recognized hound color is acceptable and the distribution of color and markings is of no importance.

DISQUALIFICATIONS

Height of more than 15 inches at the highest point of the shoulder blades. Knuckled over front legs.

Distinctly long coat.

Ch. Santana-Mandeville's Ichabod is a superb example of excellent type, soundness, and perfect proportion. Ichabod's wins include a Best of Breed and Group 4 at 10 months of age; Winners Dog, Best of Winners, and Best of Show at the Northern California Specialty; and Winners Dog and Best of Winners at Hartford. Bred, owned, and handled by Mrs. Paul E. Nelson.

Overleaf: →
Ch. Honeytree's Teddy Bear, by Ch. Musicland's Houdini ex Honeytree's Peppermint Patty, is a Best in Show and multiple Group winner, shown on a limited basis and handled by Stan Flowers. Owned by Mike and Suzy Holm, Honeytree Bassets, Buffalo, Minnesota.

135

Eng. Ch. Brackenacre Primrose (Witchacre Jim Lad ex Brackenacre Diamond Lil), Hound Group winner, Best in Show winner, Multiple Best of Breed winner. Owned by Mrs. T. Polkinghome and Mr. and Mrs. J.F.C. Nixon.

British Standard

GENERAL CHARACTERISTICS: A short-legged hound of considerable substance, well-balanced and full of quality. Action is most important. A smooth free action with forelegs reaching well forward and hind legs showing powerful thrust and the hound moving true both front and rear. Hocks and stifles must not be stiff in movement nor must any toes be dragged.

← **Overleaf:**
Ch. Northwoods' Banana Peal, by Ch. Tal-E-Ho's Top Banana ex
Ch. Galway Teresa, bred by Peter C.J. Martin, co-owned with Heidi
Martin, Northwoods Bassets, Libertyville, Illinois. Best of Opposite
Sex at the Fall National Specialty of the Basset Hound Club of
America in 1978.

HEAD AND SKULL: Domed, with some stop and the occipital bone prominent; of medium width at the brow and tapering slightly to the muzzle; the general appearance of the foreface is lean but not snipy. The top of the muzzle nearly parallel with the line from stop to occiput and not much longer than the head from stop to occiput. There may be a moderate amount of wrinkle at the brows and beside the eyes and in any event the skin of the head should be so loose as to wrinkle noticeably when drawn forward or when the head is lowered. The flews of the upper lip overlap the lower substantially.

NOSE: Entirely black, except in light-coloured hounds, when it may be brown or liver. Large with well opened nostrils and may protrude a little beyond the lips.

EYES: Brown, but may shade to hazel in light-coloured hounds, neither prominent nor too deep set. The expression is calm and serious and the red of the lower lid appears, though not exceedingly.

EARS: Set on low but not excessively so and never above the line of the eye, very long, reaching at least to the end of a muzzle of correct length, narrow throughout their length and curling well inwards; very supple, fine and velvety in texture.

MOUTH: The teeth level with a scissors bite although if they meet edge to edge it is not a fault.

NECK: Muscular and fairly long with pronounced dewlap but not exaggerated.

FOREQUARTERS: Shoulder-blades well laid-back and shoulders not heavy. Forelegs short, powerful and with great bone, the elbows turned neither out nor in but fitting easily against the side. The knees at least slightly crooked inwards but not to so great an extent as to prevent free action or to result in legs touching each other when standing or in action. Knuckling-over is a bad fault. There may be wrinkles of skin between knee and foot.

BODY: The breast bone slightly prominent but the chest not narrow or unduly deep; the ribs well-rounded and sprung and carried well

Overleaf: →
Ch. Brendans Brian Boru, by Ch. Halcyon Crackerjack ex Ch. Brendan's Virginia of Tara, taking Best of Breed at Ox Ridge Kennel Club in 1983 under judge Pat Laurans. Handled by Nancy Sheehan Martin for Brasstax Bassets, Gloria Seifman, Stony Brook, New York.

back. The back rather broad, level, and with withers and quarters of approximately the same height, though the loins may arch slightly. The back from withers to the inset of the quarters not unduly long.

HINDQUARTERS: Full of muscle and standing out well, giving an almost spherical effect when viewing the hound from the rear. Stifles well bent. The hocks as low to the ground as possible and lightly bent under the hound but not turned in or out. They should be placed just under the body when standing naturally. One or two wrinkles of skin may appear between hock and foot and at the rear of the joint a slight pouch resulting from the looseness of the skin.

FEET: Massive, well knuckled-up and padded. The forefeet may point straight ahead or be turned slightly outwards but in every case the hound must stand perfectly true, the weight being borne equally by toes with pads together so that the feet would leave the imprint of a large hound and no unpadded areas in contact with the ground.

TAIL: Well set-on, rather long, strong at the base and tapering with a moderate amount of coarse hair underneath. When the hound is moving the stern is carried well up and curves gently sabre-fashion over the back but is never curling or gay.

COAT: Smooth, short and close without being too fine. The whole outline should be clean and free from feathering. The presence of a long-haired soft coat, with feathering, is very undesirable.

COLOUR: Generally black, white and tan or lemon and white, but any recognised hould color is acceptable.

HEIGHT: Height 33-38 cm (13"-15").

FAULTS: Any departure from the foregoing points should be considered a fault and the seriousness with which the fault should be regarded should be in exact proportion to its degree.

←Overleaf:
(Top) Ch. Orange Park Grover with handler Jerry Rigden. One of the breed's great dogs of the early 1970's. Owned by Oranpark Kennels, the Meyers, Orange, California. *(Bottom)* Invaluable photograph of the two Bassets who dominated the breed for half a decade during the late 1970's. *(Left)* Champion Strathalbyn Shoot To Kill, C.D., T.D. and *(right)* Am. and Can. Ch. Beartooth Victor, at Aspen in 1980. Photo courtesy of Eric George.

Chapter 8

The Basset as a Family Member

The Basset Hound makes a truly super choice as a household companion, having much to offer in the area of being easy to live with, endearing and amusing in character, attractive in looks, and a good "doer."

Bassets first came widely to the attention of the general public by way of television. A lovely Basset named Cleo took the hearts of America by storm as one of the stars, along with Jackie Coogan, of the highly popular weekly "situation comedy" program, "The People's Choice." In the same general period, a Basset named Morgan was making frequent appearances on variety programs, especially "The Garry Moore Show." Suddenly everyone simply had to have one of these unique and adorable dogs, preferably one "just like Cleo" or "just like Morgan."

"Hush Puppies," for what must be at least several decades, has used a Basset as identification for its shoes, the result being posters and pictures of "The Hush Puppy Basset" everywhere. Stuffed toys have appeared in the form of Bassets. If the Basset Fancy itself had tried to launch a popularity campaign for their breed (which, I hasten to add, they have *not*), they would have found it impossible to do a better job.

The nicest thing about it all is that Bassets live up to the impression they create. They are easy-going and intelligent, love human companionship, and fit in well under almost any circumstances. Their short legs make excessive exercise unnecessary, a boon to city-dwellers. Their keen nose and excited interest as they move along make them fun to enjoy the outdoors with in the suburbs or country. Their casual and easy-going attitude makes them pleasant and relaxing to have around you in the home. And their deep, musical voices are impressive

Marlow Leigh's Holy Moses, C.D. looks proud, indeed, sporting, with perfect balance, the last word in fashionable hats. We love his solemn expression as he does so! Owned by Jacqueline Adams, Newtown, Conn. and LaVerne Anderson, Bryant, Ark. Moses earned his C.D. title at 10 years of age.

and should make trespassers think twice about coming onto premises where one is around.

Their gentle good nature, plus their lowness to the ground, make them agreeable companions for children, with whom their patience seems endless. They are strong, solid dogs, so they are not easily hurt when played with by children. And they are pack dogs who have lived with other animals since early times, so generally they are not trouble-makers or inclined to fight.

Overleaf:
Am., Can., and Bda. Ch. Webbridge Banner Bound, well-known winner of the late 1960's, owned by Patricia Fellman, Pompano Beach, Florida.

Three handsome Bassets owned by Jacqueline Adams, Newtown, Conn., and LaVerne Anderson, Bryant, Ark. Left to right, Ch. Placid Farm's King Solumn-Un, C.D.; Ch. Placid Farm's B-U-Tiful Beaulah; and right Ch. Baskerville's Happy Tracks, with handler Barbara Brannon.

Overleaf: →

(Top) It's not every Basset that can win a Specialty at age 11 years! Here's Ch. Glenhaven Lord Jack doing exactly that, at the Basset Hound Club of Greater Corpus Christi, in 1978. Owner-handled by Hettie Page Garwood, judged by Robert B. Booth. Trophy presented by Palmer (Pat) Glenn. *(Bottom)* Ch. Beaujangle's Ten, ROM. by Ch. Beaujangle's Mr. Mustard ex Belyn's Jezabel of Beaujangle, a Best in Show winner owned by Claudia Lane and Diane Malenfant.

English Champions Brackenacre James Bond, Brackenacre The Viking, Brackenacre Primrose, and Brackenacre Jessica relaxing at home. Owned by Mr. and Mrs. J.F.C. Nixon, Plymouth, Devon, England.

Their appetites are hearty and cause no problems for their owners. They walk politely on lead, not lurching and pulling at everything they see as do some of the more active breeds. They are affectionate and docile, particularly happy when permitted to stretch out and nap on the couch. They are nice dogs for the city as they give the impression of being small dogs owing to their short legs, but they are massive and heavy for their size and they have all the true "dogginess" one likes to find in a canine companion.

The Basset is quite a clown and seems to know it, basking in the face of your amusement at his antics. He is not by nature destructive.

Since they are a short-coated breed, Bassets are no grooming problem. A thorough rubdown with a "hound mitt" (available from your pet supplier) will keep his coat clean and shining, as will a thorough drying with a large turkish towel when he comes in wet from outdoors. Frequent bathing is unnecessary if you make sure the two "rubdowns" are done routinely.

← **Overleaf:**
Ch. Joan Urban's Strathalbyn El Al, born July 1977, by Ch. Strathalbyn Shoot to Kill ex Ch. Joan Urbans Etc of Tantivy is owned by Joan Urban, was bred and handled by Eric George.

Chapter 9

The Purchase of Your Dog or Puppy

Careful consideration should be given to what breed of dog you wish to own prior to your purchase of one. If several breeds are attractive to you, and you are undecided which you prefer, learn all you can about the characteristics of each before making your decision. As you do so, you are thus preparing yourself to make an intelligent choice; and this is very important when buying a dog who will be, with reasonable luck, a member of your household for at least a dozen years or more. Obviously since you are reading this book, you have decided on the breed—so now all that remains is to make a good choice.

It is never wise to just rush out and buy the first cute puppy who catches your eye. Whether you wish a dog to show, one with whom to compete in obedience, or one as a family dog purely for his (or her) companionship, the more time and thought you invest as you plan the purchase, the more likely you are to meet with complete satisfaction. The background and early care behind your pet will reflect in the dog's future health and temperament. Even if you are planning the purchase purely as a pet, with no thoughts of showing or breeding in

Overleaf: →
Ch. Strathalbyn War Paint, by Strathalbyn Hathaway ex Strathalbyn Coldstream Gina, was bred by Erica V. George, M.D. This multi-Group winner, line-bred with heavy influence on Ch. Lyn-Mar Acres M'Lord Batuff, is pictured with Eric George making a Group placement in 1983.

Ch. Windmaker's Bermuda High, taking Best of Winners at Thronateeska K.C. in 1981. Bred and owned by James R. and Wanda White, Mrs. White handling, Windmaker Bassets, Hickory, North Carolina.

the dog's or puppy's future, it is essential that if the dog is to enjoy a trouble-free future you assure yourself of a healthy, properly raised puppy or adult from sturdy, well-bred stock.

Throughout the pages of this book you will find the names and locations of many well-known and well-established kennels in various areas. Another source of information is the American Kennel Club (51 Madison Avenue, New York, NY 10010) from whom you can obtain a list of recognized breeders in the vicinity of your home. If you plan to have your dog campaigned by a professional handler, by all means let the handler help you locate and select a good dog. Through their numerous clients, handlers have access to a variety of interesting show prospects; and the usual arrangement is that the handler re-sells the dog to you for what his cost has been, with the agreement that the dog be campaigned for you by him throughout the dog's career. It is most strongly recommended that prospective purchasers follow these suggestions, as you thus will be better able to locate and select a satisfactory puppy or dog.

Your first step in searching for your puppy is to make appointments at kennels specializing in the chosen breed, where you can visit and inspect the dogs, both those available for sale and the kennel's basic breeding stock. You are looking for an active, sturdy puppy with bright eyes and intelligent expression and who is friendly and alert; avoid puppies who are hyperactive, dull, or listless. The coat should be clean and thick, with no sign of parasites. The premises on which he was raised should look (and smell) clean and be tidy, making it obvious that the puppies and their surroundings are in capable hands. Should the kennels featuring the breed you intend owning be sparse in your area or not have what you consider attractive, do not hesitate to contact others at a distance and purchase from them if they seem better able to supply a puppy or dog who will please you *so long as it is a recognized breeding kennel of that breed*. Shipping dogs is a regular practice nowadays, with comparatively few problems when one considers the number of dogs shipped each year. A reputable, well-known breeder wants the customer to be satisfied; thus he will represent the puppy fairly. Should you not be pleased with the puppy upon arrival, a breeder such as one described above will almost certainly permit its return. A conscientious breeder takes real interest and concern in the welfare of the dogs he or she causes to be brought into the world. Such a breeder also is proud of a reputation for integrity. Thus on two counts, for the sake of the dog's future and the breeder's reputation, to such a person a *satisfied* customer takes precedence over a sale at any cost.

If your puppy is to be a pet or "family dog," the earlier the age at which it joins your household the better. Puppies are weaned and ready to start out on their own, under the care of a sensible new owner, at about six weeks old; and if you take a young one, it is often easier to train it to the routine of your household and your requirements of it than is the case with an older dog which, even though still a puppy

The magnificent and consistent winner, Champion Talleyrand's Keene winning the Long Island Basset Hound Club Specialty in Sept. 1964. Owned by Mr. and Mrs. Robert Ellenberger.

Overleaf: →
Ch. Brendans Archdeacon, a consistent Group winner currently, is by Ch. Tal-E-Ho's Jet, C.D.X. ex Ch. Brendans Vanessa. Handled by Doug Holloway for John and Anne D. O'Reilly, Camp Hill, PA. Pictured winning the Hound Group at Forsyth Kennel Club in 1982.

technically, may have already started habits you will find difficult to change. The younger puppy is usually less costly, too, as it stands to reason the breeder will not have as much expense invested in it. Obviously, a puppy that has been raised to five or six months old represents more in care and cash expenditure on the breeder's part than one sold earlier and therefore should be and generally is priced accordingly.

There is an enormous amount of truth in the statement that "bargain" puppies seldom turn out to be that. A "cheap" puppy, cheaply raised purely for sale and profit, can and often does lead to great heartbreak including problems and veterinarian's bills which can add up to many times the initial cost of a properly reared dog. On the other hand, just because a puppy is expensive does not assure one that is healthy and well reared. Numerous cases are known where unscrupulous dealers have sold for several hundred dollars puppies that were sickly, in poor condition, and such poor specimens that the breed of which they were supposedly members was barely recognizable. So one cannot always judge a puppy by price alone. Common sense must guide a prospective purchaser, plus the selection of a *reliable,* well-recommended dealer whom you know to have well-satisfied customers or, best of all, a specialized breeder. You will probably find the fairest pricing at the kennel of a breeder. Such a person, experienced with the breed in general and with his or her own stock in particular, through extensive association with these dogs has watched enough of them mature to have obviously learned to assess quite accurately each puppy's potential—something impossible where such background is non-existent.

One more word on the subject of pets. Bitches make a fine choice for this purpose as they are usually quieter and more gentle than the males, easier to house train, more affectionate, and less inclined to

← **Overleaf:**
(Top) Ch. Lyn Mar Acres Joker's Wild, multiple Best in Show and Hound Group winner, by Ch. Lyn Mar Acres M'Lord Batuff ex Flareout Aria (an English import). Joker was a litter-brother to Ch. Lyn Mar Acres April Showers who finished undefeated for Winners Bitch, owner-handled by Mrs. Margaret S. Walton. Joker's Wild was finished to his title by Roy Murray handling for Mrs. Walton, then leased for his show career to Mrs. Patricia Kapplow, Delmas Kennels. *(Bottom)* Ch. Lyn Mar Acres V.I.P. winning the Group after having won the Basset Hound Club of America Spring Specialty from the classes. By Lyn Mar Acres Lord Hyssop (son of Batuff) ex Flareout Aria. Bred and owned by Margaret S. Walton. Handled by Roy Murray.

Ch. Forestbay's Lonesome George, owned by Mr. and Mrs. Joseph Kulper, Forestbay Kennels. One of the important Bassets of the 1960s. Handled by Dorothy Hardy; photo from the collection of the late Dorothy and Frank Hardy.

Overleaf: →
Ch. Wagtails Rise and Shine snapped informally with handler
Roberta Campbell. Winner of Group placements, owned by Mr.
and Mrs. Alfred A. Wicklund and Mary Louise Chipman. John
Ashbey took this beautiful photo.

159

My Lu's Sunshine Shirley, C.D. owned by Louisa A. Myers, and Het's Here Comes The General, C.D., co-owned by Het Garwood and Louisa A. Myers, winning 1st and 2nd places in the Veteran's Obedience, Basset Hound Club of America National Specialty, Dallas, Texas, October 1980. These two also won the Brace Obedience Class.

← **Overleaf:**
A delightful informal photo of the great Ch. Strathalbyn Shoot To Kill, C.D., T.D. (left) with Ch. Strathalbyn Court Affair. Shoot To Kill is the breed's first Top Winning Basset (1979) to hold both obedience and tracking titles as well; and the only member of a registered Basset pack to win Best in Show. Bred by Eric F. George, owned by Kay and Craig Green, Littleton, Colorado.

roam. If you do select a bitch and have no intention of breeding or showing her, by all means have her spayed, for your sake and for hers. The advantages to the owner of a spayed bitch include avoiding the nuisance of "in season" periods which normally occur twice yearly, with the accompanying eager canine swains haunting your premises in an effort to get close to your female, plus the unavoidable messiness and spotting of furniture and rugs at this time, which can be annoying if she is a household companion in the habit of sharing your sofa or bed. As for the spayed bitch, she benefits as she grows older because this simple operation almost entirely eliminates the possibility of breast cancer ever occurring. The consensus is that all bitches should eventually be spayed—even those used for show or breeding when their careers are ended—in order that they may enjoy a happier healthier old age. Please take note, however, that a bitch who has been spayed (or an altered dog) *cannot be shown at American Kennel Club Dog shows once this operation has been performed.* Be certain that you are *not* interested in showing her before taking this step.

Also in selecting a pet, never underestimate the advantages of an older dog, perhaps a retired show dog or a bitch no longer needed for breeding, who may be available quite reasonably priced by a breeder anxious to place such a dog in a loving home. These dogs are settled and can be a delight to own, as they make wonderful companions, especially in a household of adults where raising a puppy can sometimes be a trial.

Everything we have said about careful selection of your pet puppy and its place of purchase applies, but with many further considerations, when you plan to buy a show dog or foundation stock for a future breeding program. Now is the time for an in-depth study of the breed, starting with every word and every illustration in this book and all others you can find written on the subject. The standard of the breed now has become your guide, and you must learn not only the words but also how to interpret them and how they are applicable in actual dogs before you are ready to make an intelligent selection of a show dog.

Overleaf: →
The Best in Show winning Am. and Can. Ch. Harper's Bart of Parkside, by Ch. Harper's Rhett Butler ex Lindsay's Sober Sister, bred by Tom and Medora Harper, owned by Ivan and Phyllis Macklin, Winnipeg, Manitoba. He was No. 1 Basset in Canada for 1975 and No. 7 among all Hounds.

Can. and Am. Ch. Chantinghall Blockbuster, by Can. and Am. Ch. Chantinghall
Dominic ex Chantinghall Mary Kate. The Top Basset Male in all of Canada for
1980, bred by Liz Lors, owned by Rosemary McKnight, Chantinghall Bassets,
Wainfleet, Ontario, Canada.

Ch. The Ring's Banshee, by Ch. Seifenjagenheim's Lazy Boy ex Ch. Lyn Mar Acres Flirtation, bred by Mr. and Mrs. Robert Noerr, owned by Mr. Chris Teeter. From the collection of the late Frank and Dorothy Hardy.

Ch. Slowpoke Hubertus, by Ch. Hartshead Pepper ex Abigail of Woodleigh, bred by Isabel A. Holden, owned by Chris Teeter, handled by Frank Hardy. From the collection of the late Dorothy and Frank Hardy.

If you are thinking in terms of a dog to show, obviously you must have learned about dog shows and must be in the habit of attending them. This is fine, but now your activity in this direction should be increased, with your attending every single dog show within a reasonable distance from your home. Much can be learned about a breed at ringside at these events. Talk with the breeders who are exhibiting. Study the dogs they are showing. Watch the judging with concentration, noting each decision made and attempt to follow the reasoning by which the judge has reached it. Note carefully the attributes of the dogs who win and, for your later use, the manner in which each is presented. Close your ears to the ringside know-it-alls, usually novice owners of only a dog or two and very new to the fancy, who have only derogatory remarks to make about all that is taking place unless they happen to win. This is the type of exhibitor who "comes and goes" through the fancy and whose interest is usually of very short duration owing to lack of knowledge and dissatisfaction caused by the failure to recognize the need to learn. You, as a fancier who we hope will last and enjoy our sport over many future years, should develop independent thinking at this stage; you should learn to draw your own conclusions about the merits, or lack of them, seen before you in the ring and thus, sharpen your own judgment in preparation for choosing wisely and well.

Note carefully which breeders campaign winning dogs, not just an occasional isolated good one but consistent, homebred winners. It is from one of these people that you should select your own future "star."

If you are located in an area where dog shows take place only occasionally or where there are long travel distances involved, you will need to find another testing ground for your ability to select a worthy show dog. Possibly, there are some representative kennels raising this breed within a reasonable distance. If so, by all means ask permission of the owners to visit the kennels and do so when permission is granted. You may not necessarily buy then and there, as they may not have available what you are seeking that very day, but you will be able to see the type of dog being raised there and to discuss the dogs with the breeder. Every time you do this, you add to your knowledge. Should one of these kennels have dogs which especially appeal to you, perhaps you could reserve a show-prospect puppy from a coming litter. This is frequently done, and it is often worth waiting for a puppy, unless you have seen a dog with which you are truly greatly impressed and which is immediately available.

Brackenacre Crystal Clear
(Ch. Brackenacre the
Viking ex Pendlewitch of
Brackenacre) at three
months old, a week before
being exported to Sweden.
Bred by Brackenacre
Bassets, Mr. and Mrs.
J.F.C. Nixon, Plymouth,
Devon, England.

Ch. Branscombe Bianca,
T.D., owned by Francis and
Ruth Paule, Branscombe,
Riverton, Indiana.

We have already discussed the purchase of a pet puppy. Obviously this same approach applies in a far greater degree when the purchase involved is a future show dog. The only place at which to purchase a show prospect is from a breeder who raises show-type stock; otherwise, you are almost certainly doomed to disappointment as the puppy matures. Show and breeding kennels obviously cannot keep all of their fine young stock. An active breeder-exhibitor is, therefore, happy to place promising youngsters in the hands of people also interested in showing and winning with them, doing so at a fair price according to the quality and prospects of the dog involved. Here again, if no kennel in your immediate area has what you are seeking, do not hesitate to contact top breeders in other areas and to buy at long distance. Ask for pictures, pedigrees, and a complete description. Heed the breeder's advice and recommendations, after truthfully telling exactly what your expectations are for the dog you purchase. Do you want something with which to win just a few ribbons now and then? Do you want a dog who can complete his championship? Are you thinking of the real "big time" (*i.e.*, seriously campaigning with Best of Breed, Group wins, and possibly even Best in Show as your eventual goal)? Consider it all carefully in advance; then honestly discuss your plans with the breeder. You will be better satisfied with the results if you do this, as the breeder is then in the best position to help you choose the dog who is most likely to come through for you. A breeder selling a show dog is just as anxious as the buyer for the dog to succeed, and the breeder will represent the dog to you with truth and honesty. Also, this type of breeder does not lose interest the moment the sale has been made but when necessary will be right there ready to assist you with beneficial advice and suggestions based on years of experience.

As you make inquiries of at least several kennels, keep in mind that show-prospect puppies are less expensive than mature show dogs, the latter often costing close to four figures, and sometimes more. The reason for this is that, with a puppy, there is always an element of chance, the possibility of its developing unexpected faults as it

← **Overleaf:**
(Top) Sagaces Corker, littermate to Sagaces Charity, Clarrie, Casper, and Conroy, by Aust. Ch. Hushanda Kid Gloves ex Aust. Ch. Sagaces Harmony. *(Bottom)* Aust. Ch. Sagaces Major Dundee is brother to Aust. Ch. Sagaces Merryman and Reserve Best in Show and Best Hound Exhibit winner. Both Bassets pictured were bred and owned by Sue and Barry Millar, Sydney, Australia.

Brewerscote The Norfeman of Orakei, owned by Miss Frances Muirhead, Orakei, Cromer, Norfolk, England. Bred by Mrs. Hughes, Norfeman is by Eng. Ch. Brackenacre The Viking ex Eng. Ch. Bezel Isabella.

Overleaf: →
Ch. Windmaker's Summer Thunder, by Ch. Lochopt's Halcyon Collegian ex Ch. Windmaker's Sadman Connie, bred and owned by James R. and Wanda A. White, Hickory, North Carolina.

GROUP 3RD
CHARLESTON
KENNEL CLUB INC
SEPT 1983

Ch. Beaujangle's J.P. Beauregarde, by Ch. Beaujangle's Ten ex Ch. Stephie Jane
P. Beauregarde. Owners, Claudia Lane and Diane Malenfant, Glendale, Arizona.

A magnificent head study of Jagersven Town Crier, by Bats from Jagersven Gigi, bred and owned by Finn and Mary Louise Bergishagen.

matures or failing to develop the excellence and quality that earlier had seemed probable. There definitely is a risk factor in buying a show-prospect puppy. Sometimes all goes well, but occasionally the swan becomes an ugly duckling. Reflect on this as you consider available puppies and young adults. It just might be a good idea to go with a more mature, though more costly, dog if one you like is available.

When you buy a mature show dog, "what you see is what you get"; and it is not likely to change beyond coat and condition which are dependent on your care. Also advantageous for a novice owner is the fact that a mature dog of show quality almost certainly will have received show ring training and probably match show experience, which will make your earliest handling ventures far easier.

Frequently it is possible to purchase a beautiful dog who has completed championship but who, owing to similarity in bloodlines, is not needed for the breeder's future program. Here you have the opportunity of owning a champion, usually in the two- to five-year-old range, which you can enjoy campaigning as a "special" (for Best of Breed competition) and which will be a settled, handsome dog for you and your family to enjoy with pride.

If you are planning foundation for a future kennel, concentrate on acquiring one or two really superior bitches. These need not necessarily be top show-quality, but they should represent your breed's finest producing bloodlines from a strain noted for producing quality, generation after generation. A proven matron who is already the dam of show-type puppies is, of course, the ideal selection; but these are usually difficult to obtain, no one being anxious to part with so valuable an asset. You just might strike it lucky, though, in which case you are off to a flying start. If you cannot find such a matron available, select a young bitch of finest background from top producing lines who is herself of decent type, free of obvious faults, and of good quality.

Great attention should be paid to the pedigree of the bitch from whom you intend to breed. If not already known to you, try to see the sire and dam. It is generally agreed that someone starting with a breed should concentrate on a fine collection of top-flight bitches and raise a

Overleaf: →
Ch. Limavady's Bill of Cotton Hill, bred by Elizabeth W. Redmond, owned by Edmund P. Hammond, here taking Best of Breed at Farmington Kennel Club, July 1973, under judge Joseph Kulper, handled by Edmund P. Hammond.

B.O.B.

photo by Gilbert

Ch. Coldstream Talleyrand Duffi, by Ch. Talleyrand's Keene ex Coldstream April, a homebred owned by Mr. and Mrs. Joseph McKenna, Coldstream Kennels. This hound hunted regularly with the Coldstream Pack, as did his dam and her sire and dam. Handled by Dorothy Hardy. Photo from the collection of the late Frank and Dorothy Hardy.

few litters from these before considering keeping one's own stud dog. The practice of buying a stud and then breeding everything you own or acquire to that dog does not always work out well. It is better to take advantage of the many noted sires who are available to be used at stud, who represent all of the leading strains, and in each case carefully to select the one who in type and pedigree seems most compatible to each of your bitches, at least for your first several litters.

178

To summarize, if you want a "family dog" as a companion, it is best to buy it young and raise it to the habits of your household. If you are buying a show dog, the more mature it is, the more certain you can be of its future beauty. If you are buying foundation stock for a kennel, then bitches are better, but they must be from the finest *producing* bloodlines.

When you buy a pure-bred dog that you are told is eligible for registration with the American Kennel Club, you are entitled to receive from the seller an application form which will enable you to register your dog. If the seller cannot give you the application form you should demand and receive an identification of your dog consisting of the name of the breed, the registered names and numbers of the sire and dam, the name of the breeder, and your dog's date of birth. If the litter of which your dog is a part is already recorded with the American Kennel Club, then the litter number is sufficient identification.

Do not be misled by promises of papers at some later date. Demand a registration application form or proper identification as described above. If neither is supplied, do not buy the dog. So warns the American Kennel Club, and this is especially important in the purchase of show or breeding stock.

At the Dal-Tex Basset Hound Club, Nov. 1971, Parade of Obedience and Tracking title holders. *Left to right*, Louisa A. Myers with Ch. Hiflite's Big John, T.D.; Pat Willer with Willer's King Rufus, C.D.; Marge Cook with Nancy Evans Pandora, U.D.T.; Jeanette Woodward with Marjourie's Mr. Clyde, C.D.; Nell Looper with Marge and Jim Cook's Ch. Le Clair's Merry Madelyn, U.D.; and Cathy Anen with Bevlec's Miss Peach, C.D. Note some of today's active conformation, tracking, and field fanciers pictured!

Ch. Slippery Hill Hudson, a Top Winning Basset: 30 Bests in Show; No. 1 Basset in the U.S., 1974-1977; No. 1 Hound, 1975; Best of Breed at Westminster, 1975-1977; Winner of 1975 Ken-L-Ration Award for Hounds. Bred by Dr. and Mrs. Leonard Skolnick; owned by Mrs. Alan Robson; handled exclusively by Bobby Barlow.

Ch. Slippery Hill Daddy Warbucks, T.D., Winners Dog at Langley K.C. 1981. Owned by the Leonard Skolnicks, Harwood, Maryland.

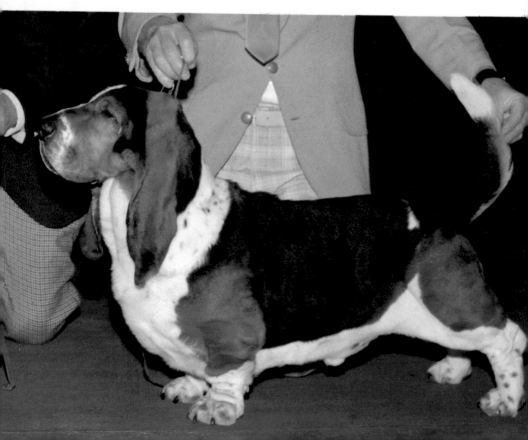

Ch. Handyman of Cape Cod, with his handler Robert s. Forsyth, owned by Louise J. and Ray D. Wells, Jr., North Harwich, Mass. Photo courtesy of Mr. Forsyth.

← Overleaf:
(Top) These are the famous Timber Ridge Basset Pack at the Bryn Mawr Hound Show in 1984. Amelia F. Rogers, Hampstead, Maryland, Master and Huntsman. *(Bottom)* Timber Ridge entry, Windmaker's South Wind, by Gorham's Southern Gentleman ex Ch. Keitham Windy, at Bryn Mawr Hound Show 1981, 1st Brood Bitch. 1st 2-couple Bassets. Champion Bitch. Champion A.K.C. Basset.

Chapter 10

The Care of Your Basset Puppy

Preparing for Your Puppy's Arrival

The moment you decide to be the new owner of a puppy is not one second too soon to start planning for the puppy's arrival in your home. Both the new family member and you will find the transition period easier if your home is geared in advance for the arrival.

The first things to be prepared are a bed for the puppy and a place where you can pen him up for rest periods. Every dog should have a crate of its own from the very beginning, so that he will come to know and love it as his special place where he is safe and happy. It is an ideal arrangement, for when you want him to be free, the crate stays open. At other times you can securely latch it and know that the pup is safely out of mischief. If you travel with him, his crate comes along in the car; and, of course, in travelling by plane there is no alternative but to have a carrier for the dog. If you show your dog, you will want him upon occasion to be in a crate a good deal of the day. So from every consideration, a crate is a very sensible and sound investment in your puppy's future safety and happiness and for your own peace of mind.

The crates recommended are the wooden ones with removable side panels, which are ideal for cold weather (with the panels in place to keep out drafts) and in hot weather (with the panels removed to allow

Overleaf: →
The noted sire and show dog, Can. and Am. Ch. Chantinghall Dominic, sire of 18 champions. Bred and owned by Rosemary McKnight, Wainfleet, Ontario, Canada.

183

better air circulation). Wire crates are all right in the summer, but they give no protection from cold or drafts. Aluminum crates are undesirable due to the manner in which aluminum reflects surrounding temperatures. If it is cold, so is the metal of the crate; if it is hot, the crate becomes burning hot. For this reason aluminum crates are neither comfortable nor safe.

When you choose the puppy's crate, be certain that it is roomy enough not to become outgrown. The crate should have sufficient height so the dog can stand up in it as a mature dog and sufficient area so that he can stretch out full length when relaxed. When the puppy is young, first give him shredded newspaper as a bed; the papers can be replaced with a mat or turkish towels when the dog is older. Carpet remnants are great for the bottom of the crate, as they are inexpensive and in case of accidents can be quite easily replaced. As the dog matures and is past the chewing age, a pillow or blanket in the crate is an appreciated comfort.

Sharing importance with the crate is a safe area in which the puppy can exercise and play. If you are an apartment dweller, a baby's playpen for a toy dog or a young puppy works out well; for a larger breed or older puppy use a portable exercise pen which you can then use later when traveling with your dog or for dog shows. If you have a yard, an area where he can be outside in safety should be fenced in prior to the dog's arrival at your home. This area does not need to be huge, but it does need to be made safe and secure. If you are in a suburban area where there are close neighbors, stockade fencing works out best as then the neighbors are less aware of the dog and the dog cannot see and bark at everything passing by. If you are out in the country where no problems with neighbors are likely to occur, then regular chain-link fencing is fine. For added precaution in both cases, use a row of concrete blocks or railroad ties inside against the entire bottom of the fence; this precludes or at least considerably lessens the chances of your dog digging his way out.

Be advised that if yours is a single dog, it is very unlikely that it will get sufficient exercise just sitting in the fenced area, which is what

← **Overleaf:**
(Top) Chantinghall Gridiron at 8 weeks, by Stoneybluff Homer ex Can. Ch. Gascony Chantinghall Dorcas. Bred and owned by Rosemary McKnight, Wainfleet, Ontario, Canada. *(Bottom)* Het's Betti Confetti and Senator Wally Wallbanger, T.D. at a Basset Hound Association Match Show. Owned by Roy A. David.

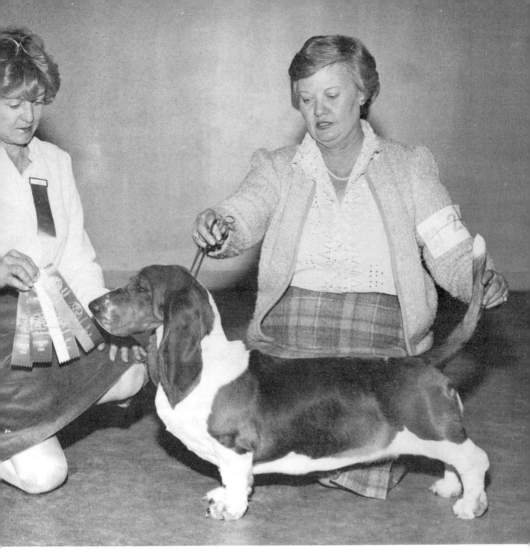

Ch. Branscombe's Comtesse Andrea, by Am. and Can. Ch. Belyn's Roustabout ex Ch. Branscombe Dulcinea, C.D., litter sister to Ch. Branscombe's Comte Richlieu, waited in the wings for her brother to finish, then took Winners Bitch both days (for majors each time) and on to Best of Breed over four Specials at the Sunday show under Mrs. Joan Urban. She finished at Tulsa, just one day over 13 months old. Handled by Judy Webb for owner Samuel Mendelson, San Francisco, California.

Overleaf: →
Am. and Can. Ch. Belyn's Roustabout, by Ch. Blue Billy Bojangles ex Belyn's Windflower, No. 1 Basset and No. 7 Hound for 1981, No. 1 Basset and No. 5 Hound in 1982 and 1983, bred by B.K. Bolch and Diane Malenfant, owned by Carolyn Bolch and handled by Judy Webb.

187

Am. and Can. Ch. Halcyon Crackerjack, ROM, holds the all-time record among Basset Hounds for Specialty Best of Breed wins. His current total of 22 Specialty Best of Breeds surpasses the previous record by over fifty percent. Owned by Gwen McCullagh and Ed Smizer, both of New Jersey.

most of them do when they are there alone. Two or more dogs will play and move themselves around, but one by itself does little more than make a leisurely tour once around the area to check things over and then lie down. You must include a daily walk or two in your plans if your puppy is to be rugged and well. Exercise is extremely important to a puppy's muscular development and to keep a mature dog fit and trim. So make sure that those exercise periods, or walks, a game of ball, and other such activities, are part of your daily program as a dog owner.

If your fenced area has an outside gate, provide a padlock and key and a strong fastening for it, and use them, so that the gate can not be opened by others and the dog taken or turned free. The ultimate convenience in this regard is, of course, a door (unused for other pur-

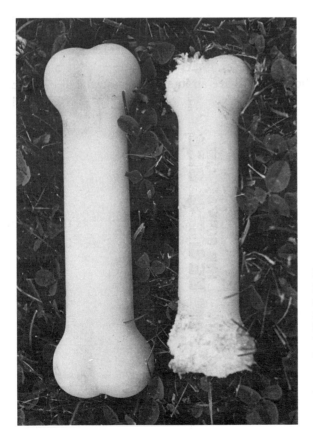

Nylabone® is now manufactured in several shapes (rings, knots, and balls) besides the traditional bone shape. This very popular pet product is available in traditional meat flavoring or chocolate flavoring as well.

poses) from the house around which the fenced area can be enclosed, so that all you have to do is open the door and out into his area he goes. This arrangement is safest of all, as then you need not be using a gate, and it is easier in bad weather since then you can send the dog out without taking him and becoming soaked yourself at the same time. This is not always possible to manage, but if your house is arranged so that you could do it this way, surely you would never regret it due to the convenience and added safety thus provided. Fencing in the entire yard, with gates to be opened and closed whenever a caller, delivery-man, postman, or some other person comes on your property, really is not safe at all because people not used to gates and their importance are frequently careless about closing and latching gates *securely*. Many heartbreaking incidents brought about by someone carelessly only half closing a gate which the owner had thought to be firmly latched and the dog wandering out are frequently reported. For greatest security a fenced *area* definitely takes precedence over a fence *yard*.

The puppy will need a collar (one that fits now, not one to be grown into) and lead from the moment you bring him home. Both should be an appropriate weight and type for his size. Also needed are a feeding dish and a water dish, both made preferably of unbreakable material. Your pet supply shop should have an interesting assortment of these and other accessories from which you can choose. Then you will need grooming tools of the type the breeder recommends and some toys. One of the best toys is a beef bone, either rib, leg, or knuckle (the latter the type you can purchase to make soup), cut to an appropriate size for your puppy dog. These are absolutely safe and are great exercise for the teething period, helping to get the baby teeth quickly out of the way with no problems. Equally satisfactory is Nylabone® , nylon bone that does not chip or splinter and that "frizzles" as the puppy chews, providing healthful gum massage. Rawhide chews are safe, too, *if made in the United States.* There was a problem a few years back owing to the chemicals with which some foreign rawhide toys had been treated, since which time we have carefully avoided giving them to our own dogs. Also avoid plastics and any sort of rubber toys, *particularly* those with squeakers which the puppy may remove and swallow. If you want a ball for the puppy to use when playing with

Overleaf: →
Ch. Manor Hills Father James, ROM, bred and owned by Ronald and Joan Scholz, Manor Hill Bassets.

191

Aberle's J.B. Buffington represents the 9th generation of Notrenom's bloodlines tracing back to Ch. Jones' Virginia Jim, C.D. By Ch. Aberle's Cral (Ch. Notrenom's Richard E ex Ch. Notrenom's Flambante Fleche) from Aberle's Arrow Too. Photo courtesy of Evelyn Bassett.

him, select one of very hard construction made for this purpose and do not leave it alone with him because he may chew off and swallow bits of the rubber. Take the ball with you when the game is over. This also applies to some of those "tug of war" type rubber toys which are fun when used with the two of you for that purpose but again should *not* be left behind for the dog to work on with his teeth. Bits of swallowed rubber, squeakers, and other such foreign articles can wreak great havoc in the intestinal tract—do all you can to guard against them.

Too many changes all at once can be difficult for a puppy. For at least the first few days he is with you, keep him on the food and feeding schedule to which he is accustomed. Find out ahead of time from the breeder what he feeds his puppies, how frequently, and at what times of the day. Also find out what, if any, food supplements the breeder has been using and recommends. Then be prepared by getting in a supply of the same food so that you will have it there when you bring the puppy home. Once the puppy is accustomed to his new sur-

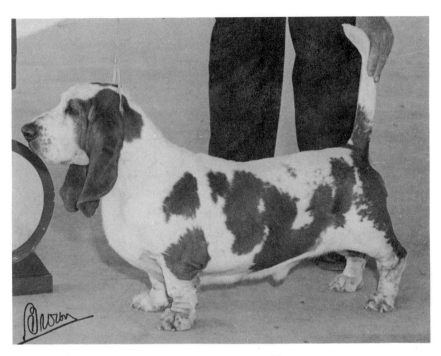

Ch. Eleandon's Mr. Pinkerton, by Eleandon's Butcher Boy ex Ch. Eleandon's Mary Lane, winning in the mid-sixties, handled by Frank Hardy. Bred by Mr. and Mrs. Donald Bliss. Owner, Mona G. Ball. Photo from the collection of the late Frank and Dorothy Hardy.

roundings, then you can switch the type of food and schedule to fit your convenience, but for the first several days do it as the puppy expects.

Your selection of a veterinarian also should be attended to before the puppy comes home, because you should stop at the vet's office for the puppy to be checked over as soon as you leave the breeder's premises. If the breeder is from your area, ask him for recommendations. Ask your dog-owning friends for their opinions of the local veterinarians, and see what their experiences with those available have been. Choose someone whom several of your friends recommend highly, then contact him about your puppy, perhaps making an appointment to stop in at his office. If the premises are clean, modern, and well equipped, and if you like the veterinarian, make an appointment to bring the puppy in on the day of purchase. Be sure to obtain the puppy's health record from the breeder, including information on such things as shots and worming that the puppy has had.

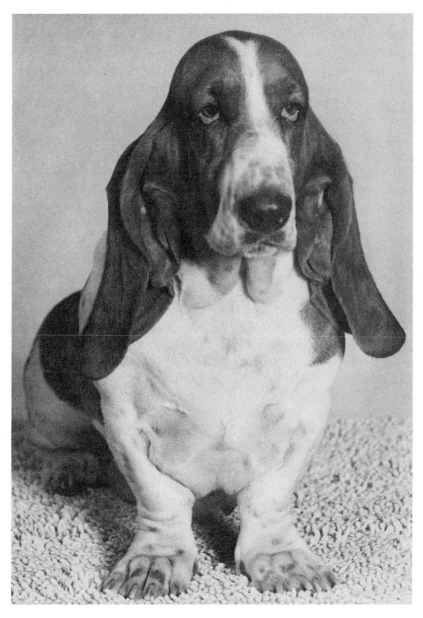

Ch. Santana-Mandeville's Sweet Pea, by Ch. Santana Count Dracula ex Pretty Penelope of Mandeville, owned by Santana-Mandeville Basset Kennels, Mr. and Mrs. Paul E. Nelson, Agoura, California. Photo courtesy of Dr. and Mrs. Leonard Skolnick.

Joining the Family

Remember that, exciting and happy an occasion as it is for you, the puppy's move from his place of birth to your home can be, for him, a traumatic experience. His mother and littermates will be missed. He quite likely will be awed or frightened by the change of surroundings. The person on whom he depended will be gone. Everything should be planned to make his arrival at your home pleasant—to give him confidence and to help him realize that yours is a pretty nice place to be after all.

Never bring a puppy home on a holiday. There just is too much going on with people and gifts and excitement. If he is in honor of an "occasion," work it out so that his arrival will be a few days earlier or, perhaps even better, a few days later than the "occasion." Then your home will be back to its normal routine and the puppy can enjoy your undivided attention. Try not to bring the puppy home in the evening. Early morning is the ideal time, as then he has the opportunity of getting acquainted and the initial strangeness should wear off before bedtime. You will find it a more peaceful night that way. Allow the puppy to investigate as he likes, under your watchful eye. If you already have a pet in the household, keep a careful watch that the relationship between the two gets off to a friendly start or you may quickly find yourself with a lasting problem. Much of the future attitude of each toward the other will depend on what takes place that first day, so keep your mind on what they are doing and let your other activities slide for the moment. Be careful not to let your older pet become jealous by paying more attention to the puppy than to him, as that will start a bad situation immediately.

If you have a child, here again it it important that the relationship start out well. Before the puppy is brought home, you should have a talk with the youngster about puppies, so that it will be clearly understood that puppies are fragile and can easily be injured; therefore, they should not be teased, hurt, mauled, or overly rough-housed. A puppy is not an inanimate toy; it is a living thing with a right to be loved and handled respectfully, treatment which will reflect in the dog's attitude toward your child as both mature together. Never permit your children's playmates to mishandle the puppy, tormenting the puppy until it turns on the children in self-defense. Children often do not realize how rough is too rough.

Do not start out by spoiling your puppy. A puppy is usually pretty smart and can be quite demanding. What you had considered to be

Dixie Hall, wife of country music star Tom T. Hall, enjoyed an exciting winning career with this outstanding Basset, Ch. Dixie's Woodpile (Ch. Dixie's Queso Grande ex Ch. Dixie's Orange Blossom) bred and handled by Mrs. Hall. Taking the breed here under judge Marcia Foy at the Macon Kennel Club in 1980.

"just for tonight" may be accepted by the puppy as "for keeps." Be firm with him, strike a routine, and stick to it. The puppy will learn more quickly this way, and everyone will be happier at the result. A radio playing softly or a dim night light are often comforting to a puppy as it gets accustomed to new surroundings and should be provided in preference to bringing the puppy to bed with you—unless, of course, you intend him to share the bed as a permanent arrangement.

Socializing and Training Your New Puppy

Socialization and training of your puppy should start the very day of his arrival in your home. Never address him without calling him by name. A short, simple name is the easiest to teach as it catches the dog's attention quickly, so avoid elaborate call names. Always address the dog by the same name, not a whole series of pet names; the latter will only confuse the puppy.

Using his name clearly, call the puppy over to you when you see him awake and wandering about. When he comes, make a big fuss over him for being such a good dog. He thus will quickly associate the sound of his name with coming to you and a pleasant happening.

Several hours after the puppy's arrival is not too soon to start accustoming him to the feel of a light collar. He may hardly notice it; or he may struggle, roll over, and try to rub it off his neck with his paws. Divert his attention when this occurs by offering a tasty snack or a toy (starting a game with him) or by petting him. Before long he will have accepted the strange feeling around his neck and no longer appear aware of it. Next comes the lead. Attach it and then immediately take the puppy outside or otherwise try to divert his attention with things to see and sniff. He may struggle against the lead at first, biting at it and trying to free himself. Do not pull him with it at this point; just hold the end loosely and try to follow him if he starts off in any direction. Normally his attention will soon turn to investigating his surroundings if he is outside or you have taken him into an unfamiliar room in your house; curiosity will take over and he will become interested in sniffing around the surroundings. Just follow him with the lead slackly held until he seems to have completely forgotten about it; then try with gentle urging to get him to follow you. Don't be rough or jerk at him; just tug gently on the lead in short quick motions (steady pulling can become a battle of wills), repeating his name or trying to get him to follow your hand which is holding a bit of food or an interesting toy. If you have an older lead-trained dog, then it should be a cinch to get the puppy to follow along after *him*. In any event, the average puppy learns quite quickly and will soon be trotting along nicely on the lead. Once that point has been reached, the next step is to teach him to follow on your left side, or heel. Of course this will not likely be accomplished all in one day but should be done with short training periods over the course of several days until you are satisfied with the result.

Brownridge Bootlegger, C.D., T.D.X., Can. T.D.X., Bda. T.D. Born August 21st 1973. Bred by Roland R. and Evelyn R. Brown, by General Sherman U.D.T. ex Brown's Lady Charmin, C.D. Owned by Thomas C. and Susan A. Boyd, St. Louis, Mo.

Dr. Byron Wisner relaxes in the hammock with Beartooth Hester.

Ch. Strathalbyn Shoot To Kill, C.D., T.D. tracking in the field. "Michael" is the only top-winning Best in Show Basset Hound to earn tracking and obedience titles as well. Eric F. George, breeder. Kay and Craig Green, owners, Littleton, Colorado.

Ch. Custusha's Mudslide Slim, on left with Robert Forsyth, owned by Dana Knowlton. On the right, Joanne Lynch with one of her many winners.

During the course of house training your puppy, you will need to take him out frequently and at regular intervals: first thing in the morning directly from the crate, immediately after meals, after the puppy has been napping, or when you notice that the puppy is looking for a spot. Choose more or less the same place to take the puppy each time so that a pattern will be established. If he does not go immediately, do not return him to the house as he will probably relieve himself the moment he is inside. Stay out with him until he has finished; then be lavish with your praise for his good behavior. If you catch the puppy having an accident indoors, grab him firmly and rush him outside, sharply saying "No!" as you pick him up. If you do not see the accident occur, there is little point in doing anything except cleaning it up, as once it has happened and been forgotten, the puppy will most likely not even realize why you are scolding him.

Especially if you live in a big city or are away many hours at a time, having a dog that is trained to go on paper has some very definite advantages. To do this, one proceeds pretty much the same way as taking the puppy outdoors, except now you place the puppy on the newspaper at the proper time. The paper should always be kept in the same spot. An easy way to paper train a puppy if you have a playpen for it or an exercise pen is to line the area with newspapers; then gradually, every day or so, remove a section of newspaper until you are down to just one or two. The puppy acquires the habit of using the paper; and as the prepared area grows smaller, in the majority of cases the dog will continue to use whatever paper is still available. My own experience, with dogs is that this works out well. It is pleasant, if the dog is alone for an excessive length of time, to be able to feel that if he needs it the paper is there and will be used.

The puppy should form the habit of spending a certain amount of time in his crate, even when you are home. Sometimes the puppy will do this voluntarily, but if not it should be taught to do so, which is accomplished by leading the puppy over by his collar, gently pushing him inside, and saying firmly "Down" or "Stay." Whatever expression you use to give a command, stick to the very same one each time for each act. Repetition is the big thing in training—and so is association with what the dog is expected to do. When you mean "Sit" always say exactly that. "Stay" should mean *only* that the dog should remain where he receives the command. "Down" means something else again. Do not confuse the dog by shuffling the commands, as this will create training problems for you.

Littermates Ch. Bugle Bay's Rhubard; Ch. Bugle Bay's Bouillon, C.D.X., T.D., ROM; and Ch. Bugle Bay's Omelet (the latter two both field pointed), are by Ch. Harper's Rhett Butler ex Ch. Bugle Bay's Much Ado Annie, C.D. Jim and Margery Cook, owners, Azle, Texas.

As soon as he has had his immunization shots, take your puppy with you whenever and wherever possible. There is nothing that will build a self-confident, stable dog like socialization, and it is extremely important that you plan and give the time and energy necessary for this whether your dog is to be a show dor or a pleasant, well-adjusted family member. Take your puppy in the car so that he will learn to enjoy riding and not become carsick as dogs may do if they are infrequent travelers. Take him anywhere you are going where you are certain he will be welcome: visiting friends and relatives (if they do not have housepets who may resent the visit), busy shopping centers (keeping him always on lead), or just walking around the streets of your town. If someone admires him (as always seems to happen when we are out with puppies), encourage the stranger to pet and talk with him. Socialization of this type brings out the best in your puppy and helps him to grow up with a friendly outlook, liking the world and its inhabitants. The worst thing that can be done to a puppy's personality is to overly shelter him. By keeping him always at home away from things and people unfamiliar to him you may be creating a personality problem for the mature dog that will be a cross for you to bear later on.

Feeding Your Dog

Time was when providing nourishing food for our dogs involved a far more complicated procedure than people now feel is necessary. The old school of thought was that the daily ration must consist of fresh beef, vegetables, cereal, egg yolks, and cottage cheese as basics with such additions as brewer's yeast and vitamin tablets on a daily basis.

During recent years, however, many minds have changed regarding this procedure. We still give eggs, cottage cheese, and supplements to the diet, but the basic method of feeding dogs has changed; and the change has been, in the opinion of many authorities, definitely for the better. The school of thought now is that you are doing your dogs a favor when you feed them some of the fine commercially prepared dog foods in preference to your own home-cooked concoctions.

The reason behind this new outlook is easily understandable. The dog food industry has grown to be a major one, participated in by some of the best known and most respected names in the American way of life. These trusted firms, it is agreed, turn out excellent products, so people are feeding their dog food preparations with confidence and the dogs are thriving, living longer, happier, and healthier lives than ever before. What more could we want?

There are at least half a dozen absolutely top-grade dry foods to be mixed with broth or water and served to your dog according to directions. There are all sorts of canned meats, and there are several kinds of "convenience foods," those in a packet which you open and dump out into the dog's dish. It is just that simple. The "convenience" foods are neat and easy to use when you are away from home, but generally speaking we prefer a dry food mixed with hot water or soup and meat. We also feel that the canned meat, with its added fortifiers, is more beneficial to the dogs than the fresh meat. However, the two can be alternated or, if you prefer and your dog does well on it, by all means use fresh ground beef. A dog enjoys changes in the meat part of his diet, which is easy with the canned food since all sorts of beef are available (chunk, ground, stewed, and so on), plus lamb, chicken, and even such concoctions as liver and egg, just plain liver flavor, and a blend of five meats.

There also is prepared food geared to every age bracket of your dog's life, from puppyhood on through old age, with special additions or modifications to make it particularly nourishing and beneficial. Our grandparents, and even our parents, never had it so good where the canine dinner is concerned, because these commercially prepared

Feeding time at Oranpark Kennels! Home of some of America's finest Bassets, these members of the family are enjoying their rations in true Hound fashion. Photo courtesy of Mrs. M.B. Meyer, Oranpark Kennels, Orange, California.

foods are tasty and geared to meeting the dog's gastronomic approval.

Additionally, contents and nutrients are clearly listed on the labels, as are careful instructions for feeding just the right amount for the size, weight, and age of each dog.

With these foods we do not feel the addition of extra vitamins is necessary, but if you do there are several kinds of those, too, that serve as taste treats as well as being beneficial. Your pet supplier has a full array of them.

Of course there is no reason not to cook up something for your dog if you would feel happier doing so. But it seems to us unnecessary when such truly satisfactory rations are available with so much less trouble and expense.

How often you feed your dog is a matter of how it works out best for you. Many owners prefer to do it once a day. Others think that two meals, each of smaller quantity, are better for the digestion and more satisfying to the dog, particularly if yours is a household member who stands around and watches preparations for the family meals. Do not overfeed. That is the shortest route to all sorts of problems. Follow directions and note carefully how your dog is looking. If your dog is overweight, cut back the quantity of food a bit. If the dog looks thin, then increase the amount. Each dog is an individual and the food intake should be adjusted to his requirements to keep him feeling and looking trim and in top condition.

From the time puppies are fully weaned until they are about twelve weeks old, they should be fed four times daily. From three months to six months of age, three meals should suffice. At six months of age the puppies can be fed two meals, and the twice daily feedings can be continued until the puppies are close to one year old, at which time feeding can be changed to once daily if desired.

If you do feed just once a day, do so by early afternoon at the latest and give the dog a snack, or biscuit or two, at bedtime.

Remember that plenty of fresh water should always be available to your puppy or dog for drinking. This is of utmost importance to his health.

Ch. Honey Tree's Teddy Bear, owned by Patrick and Suzy Holm, Buffalo, Minnesota, winning an exciting Best in Show for his breeder-owners; Richard Renihan judging; Stanley Flowers handler.

Chapter 11

The Making of a Show Dog

If you have decided to become a show dog exhibitor, you have accepted a very real and very exciting challenge. The groundwork has been accomplished with the selection of your future show prospect. If you have purchased a puppy, we assume that you have gone through all the proper preliminaries concerning good care, which should be the same if the puppy is a pet or future show dog with a few added precautions for the latter.

General Considerations

Remember the importance of keeping your future winner in trim, top condition. Since you want him neither too fat nor too thin, his appetite for his proper diet should be guarded, and children and guests should not be permitted to constantly be feeding him "goodies." The best treat of all is a small wad of raw ground beef or a packaged dog treat. To be avoided are ice cream, cake, cookies, potato chips, and other fattening items which will cause the dog to put on weight and may additionally spoil his appetite for the proper, nourishing, well-balanced diet so essential to good health and condition.

The importance of temperament and showmanship cannot possibly be overestimated. They have put many a mediocre dog across while lack of them can ruin the career of an otherwise outstanding specimen. From the day your dog joins your family, socialize him. Keep him accustomed to being with people and to being handled by people. Encourage your friends and relatives to "go over" him as the judges will in the ring so this will not seem a strange and upsetting experience. Practice showing his "bite" (the manner in which his teeth meet) quickly and deftly. It is quite simple to slip the lips apart with your fingers, and the puppy should be willing to accept this from you or the judge without struggle. This is also true of further mouth examination when necessary. Where the standard demands examination of the roof of the mouth and the tongue, accustom the dog to having his jaws opened wide in order for the judge to make this required examination. When missing teeth must be noted, again, teach the dog to permit his jaws to be opened wide and his side lips separated as judges will need to check them one or both of these ways.

Some judges prefer that the exhibitors display the dog's bite and other mouth features themselves. These are the considerate ones, who do not wish to chance the spreading of possible infection from dog to dog with their hands on each one's mouth—a courtesy particularly appreciated in these days of virus epidemics. But the old-fashioned judges still persist in doing it themselves, so the dog should be ready for either possibility.

Take your future show dog with you in the car, thus accustoming him to riding so that he will not become carsick on the day of a dog show. He should associate pleasure and attention with going in the car, or van or motor home. Take him where it is crowded: downtown, to the shops, everywhere you go that dogs are permitted. Make the expeditions fun for him by frequent petting and words of praise; do not just ignore him as you go about your errands.

Do not overly shelter your future show dog. Instinctively you may want to keep him at home where he is safe from germs or danger. This can be foolish on two counts. The first reason is that a puppy kept away from other dogs builds up no natural immunity against all the things with which he will come in contact at dog shows, so it is wiser actually to keep him well up to date on all protective shots and then let him become accustomed to being among dogs and dog owners. Also, a dog who never is among strange people, in strange places, or among strange dogs, may grow up with a shyness or timidity of spirit that will cause you real problems as his show career draws near.

Keep your show prospect's coat in immaculate condition with frequent grooming and daily brushing. When bathing is necessary, use a mild baby shampoo or whatever the breeder of your puppy may suggest. Several of the brand-name products do an excellent job. Be sure to rinse thoroughly so as not to risk skin irritation by traces of soap left behind and protect against soap entering the eyes by a drop of castor oil in each before you lather up. Use warm water (be sure it is not un-

A lovely front view of one of the Slippery Hill Bassets, as the breed should be presented to the judge. The Leonard Skolnicks, owners, Harwood, Maryland.

Judge Dee Hutchinson examining Ch. Strathalbyn Court Affair, second in line, Joy Brewster handling. Note the excellent fronts on both the two "specials" at the head of the line.

Ch. Santana-Mandeville's Ichabod, a famous Basset from the late 1960's. Photo courtesy of Dr. and Mrs. Leonard Skolnick.

comfortably hot or chillingly cold) and a good spray. A hair dryer is a real convenience and can be used for thorough drying after first blotting off the excess moisture with a turkish towel. A wad of cotton in each ear will prevent water entering the ear cavity.

Formation of mats should be watched for carefully if your breed is a heavily coated one, especially behind the ears and underneath the armpits. Toenails also should be watched and trimmed every few weeks. It is important not to permit nails to grow excessively long, as they will ruin the appearance of both the feet and pasterns.

Assuming that you will be handling the dog yourself, or even if he will be professionally handled, a few moments each day of dog show routine is important. Practice setting him up as you have seen the exhibitors do at the shows you've attended, and teach him to hold this position once you have him stacked to your satisfaction. Make the learning period pleasant by being firm but lavish in your praise when he responds correctly. Teach him to gait at your side at a moderate

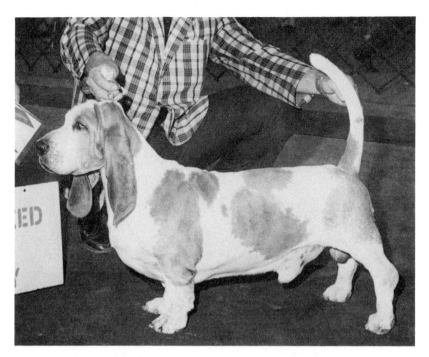

Ch. Delmas Pinkerton's Cavalier, by Ch. Eleandon's Mr. Pinkerton ex Candia's M'Lady Maude, owned and shown by Mrs. Patricia Kapplow. Pictured in 1970. Handled by Bobby Barlow.

rate on a loose lead. When you have mastered the basic essentials at home, then hunt out and join a training class for future work. Training classes are sponsored by show-giving clubs in many areas, and their popularity is steadily increasing. If you have no other way of locating one, perhaps your veterinarian would know of one through some of his other clients; but if you are sufficiently aware of the dog show world to want a show dog, you will probably be personally acquainted with other people who will share information of this type with you.

Accustom your show dog to being in a crate (which you should be doing with a pet dog as well). He should relax in his crate at the shows "between times" for his own well being and safety.

A show dog's teeth must be kept clean and free of tartar. Hard dog-biscuits can help toward this, but if tartar accumulates, see that it is removed promptly by your veterinarian. Bones are not suitable for show dogs as they tend to damage and wear down the tooth enamel.

This beautiful Basset, Ch. Crescendo's Forest O'Cock, by Ch. Forestbay Cock O'The Walk ex Crescendo's Farmer's Daughter, was born in 1976. Bred and owned by the Robert Bubbs of Highland Park, New Jersey, he finished with four majors then went on to win some Specialty Shows, including the National in 1980. Very sadly, this dog had to be put to sleep due to cancer three months after his National victory.

Match Shows

Your show dog's initial experience in the ring should be in match show competition for several reasons. First, this type of event is intended as a learning experience for both the dog and the exhibitor. You will not feel embarrassed or out of place no matter how poorly your puppy may behave or how inept your attempts at handling may be, as you will find others there with the same type of problems. The important thing is that you get the puppy out and into a show ring where the two of you can practice together and learn the ropes.

Only on rare occasions is it necessary to make match show entries in advance, and even those with a pre-entry policy will usually accept entries at the door as well. Thus you need not plan several weeks ahead, as is the case with point shows, but can go when the mood strikes you. Also there is a vast difference in the cost, as match show entries only cost a few dollars while entry fees for the point shows may be over ten dollars, an amount none of us needs to waste until we have some idea of how the puppy will behave or how much more pre-show training is needed.

Match shows very frequently are judged by professional handlers who, in addition to making the awards, are happy to help new exhibitors with comments and advice on their puppies and their presentation of them. Avail yourself of all these opportunities before heading out to the sophisticated world of the point shows.

The famous Basset bitch of the early 1960's, Champion The Ring's Banshee with her handler Frank Hardy and judge Anna Katherine Nicholas.

The noted bitch Ch. Johnson's Polyurethane owned by Robert S. Begran, Jr., has an outstanding list of important wins to her credit.

Point Shows

As previously mentioned, entries for American Kennel Club point shows must be made in advance. This must be done on an official entry blank of the show-giving club. The entry must then be filed either personally or by mail with the show superintendent or the show secretary (if the event is being run by the club members alone and a superintendent has not been hired, this information will appear on the premium list) in time to reach its destination prior to the published closing date or filling of the quota. These entries must be made carefully, must be signed by the owner of the dog or the owner's agent (your professional handler), and must be accompanied by the entry fee; other-

214

Ch. Pinedell's Erik, handsome Basset owned by Joani and Jerry Rush, Sacramento, California, receiving Best of Breed at Santa Clara Valley Kennel Club.

wise they will not be accepted. Remember that it is not when the entry leaves your hands that counts but the date of arrival at its destination. If you are relying on the mails, which are not always dependable, get the entry off well before the deadline to avoid disappointment.

A dog must be entered at a dog show in the name of the actual owner at the time of the entry closing date of that specific show. If a registered dog has been acquired by a new owner, it must be entered in the name of the new owner in any show for which entries close after the date of acquirement, regardless of whether the new owner has or has not actually received the registration certificate indicating that the dog is recorded in his name. State on the entry form whether or not transfer application has been mailed to the American Kennel Club, and it goes without saying that the latter should be attended to promptly when you purchase a registered dog.

In filling out your entry blank, type, print, or write clearly, paying particular attention to the spelling of names, correct registration numbers, and so on.

The Puppy Class is for dogs or bitches who are six months of age and under twelve months, were whelped in the United States, and are not champions. The age of a dog shall be calculated up to and inclusive of the first day of a show. For example, the first day a dog whelped on January 1st is eligible to compete in a Puppy Class at a show is July 1st of the same year; and he may continue to compete in Puppy Classes up to and including a show on December 31st of the same year, but he is *not* eligible to compete in a Puppy Class at a show held on or after January 1st of the following year.

The Puppy Class is the first one in which you should enter your puppy. In it a certain allowance will be made for the fact that they *are* puppies, thus an immature dog or one displaying less than perfect showmanship will be less severely penalized than, for instance, would be the case in Open. It is also quite likely that others in the class will be suffering from these problems, too. When you enter a puppy, be sure to check the classification with care, as some shows divide their Puppy Class into a 6-9 months old section and a 9-12 months old section.

The Novice Class is for dogs six months of age and over, whelped in the United States or Canada, who *prior to the official closing date for entires* have *not* won three first prizes in the Novice Class, any first prize at all in the Bred-by-Exhibitor, American-bred, or Open Classes, or one or more points toward championship. The provisions for this class are confusing to many people, which is probably the reason exhibitors

Gauss Duke of Cedar Hill taking points towards his title under Marcia Foy at Cen Tex Kennel Club in 1979. Gene Gauss, owner, Cedar Hill, Texas.

do not enter in it more frequently. A dog may win any number of first prizes in the Puppy Class and still retain his eligibility for Novice. He may place second, third or fourth not only in Novice on an unlimited number of occasions but also in Bred-by-Exhibitor, American-bred and Open and still remain eligible for Novice. But he may no longer be shown in Novice when he has won three blue ribbons in that class, when he has won even one blue ribbon in either Bred-by-Exhibitor, American-bred, or Open, or when he has won a single championship point.

Ch. Branscombe's Comte Richlieu, born March 1983, was a champion at 9 months and winning Best of Breed over other specials and Group placements since then. Handled by Judy Webb for owner, Samuel Mendelson, San Francisco, California. Bred by Ruth Paule and Anne Lindsay, he is a son of Am. and Can. Ch. Belyn's Roustabout ex Ch. Branscombe Dulcinea, T.D.

Ch. Coran Country Chaz, owned by Bert and Mike Salyers and Connie and Randy Frederickson. Winning a major at Dallas handled by Tracy J. Potts.

Champion Kazoo's Fredie The Freeloader owned by J. Frank Harrison, making one of his many splendid wins under Jerry Rigden's handling, this one in December 1963.

Windmaker's Summer Breeze, by Ch. Lyn-Mar Acres M'Lord Batuff ex Ch. Windmaker's Summer Storm, owned by James R. and Wanda O. White, Hickory, North Carolina.

In determining whether or not a dog is eligible for the Novice Class, keep in mind the fact that previous wins are calculated according to the official published date for closing of entries, not by the date on which you may actually have made the entry. So if in the interim, between the time you made the entry and the official closing date, your dog makes a win causing him to become ineligible for Novice, change your class *immediately* to another for which he will be eligible, preferably such as either Bred-by-Exhibitor or American-bred. To do this, you must contact the show's superintendent or secretary, at first by telephone to save time and at the same time confirm it in writing. The Novice Class always seems to have the fewest entries of any class, and therefore it is a splendid "practice ground" for you and your young dog while you are getting the "feel" of being in the ring.

Bred-by-Exhibitor Class is for dogs whelped in the United States or, if individually registered in the American Kennel Club Stud Book, for dogs whelped in Canada who are six months of age or older, are not champions, and are owned wholly or in part by the person or by the spouse of the person who was the breeder or one of the breeders of record. Dogs entered in this class must be handled in the class by an owner or by a member of the immediate family of the owner. Members of an immediate family for this purpose are husband, wife, father, mother, son, daughter, brother or sister. This is the class which is really the "breeders' showcase," and the one which breeders should enter with particular pride to show off their achievements.

The American-bred Class is for all dogs excepting champions, six months of age or older, who were whelped in the United States by reason of a mating which took place in the United States.

The Open Class is for any dog six months of age or older (this is the only restriction for this class). Dogs with championship points compete in it, dogs who are already champions are eligible to do so, dogs who are imported can be entered, and, of course, American-bred dogs compete in it. This class is, for some strange reason, the favorite of exhibitors who are "out to win." They rush to enter their pointed dogs in it, under the false impression that by doing so they assure themselves of greater attention from the judges. This really is not so, and in my opinion to enter in one of the less competitive classes, with a better chance of winning it and thus earning a second opportunity of gaining the judge's approval by returning to the ring in the Winners Class, can often be a more effective strategy.

One does not enter for the Winners Class. One earns the right to compete in it by winning first prize in Puppy, Novice, Bred-by-Exhibitor, American-bred, or Open. No dog who has been defeated on the same day in one of these classes is eligible to compete for Winners, and every dog who has been a blue-ribbon winner in one of them and not defeated in another, should he have been entered in more than one class, (as occasionally happens) *must* do so. Following the selection of the Winners Dog or the Winners Bitch, the dog or bitch receiving that award leaves the ring. Then the dog or bitch who placed second in that class, unless previously beaten by another dog or bitch in another class at the same show, re-enters the ring to compete against the remaining first-prize winners for Reserve. The latter award indicates that the dog or bitch selected for it is standing "in reserve" should the one who received Winners be disqualified or declared ineligible through any technicality when the awards are checked at the American Kennel Club. In that case, the one who placed Reserve is moved up to Winners, at the same time receiving the appropriate championship points.

Winners Dog and Winners Bitch are the awards which carry points toward championship with them. The points are based on the number of dogs or bitches actually in competition, and the points are scaled one through five, the latter being the greatest number available to any one dog or bitch at any one show. Three-, four-, or five-point wins are considered majors. In order to become a champion, a dog or bitch must have won two majors under two different judges, plus at least one point from a third judge, and the additional points necessary to bring the total to fifteen. When your dog has gained fifteen points as described above, a championship certificate will be issued to you, and your dog's name will be published in the champions of record list in the *Pure-Bred Dogs/American Kennel Gazette,* the official publication of the American Kennel Club.

The scale of championship points for each breed is worked out by the American Kennel Club and reviewed annually, at which time the number required in competition may be either changed (raised or lowered) or remain the same. The scale of championship points for all breeds is published annually in the May issue of the *Gazette,* and the current ratings for each breed within that area are published in every show catalog.

When a dog or bitch is adjudged Best of Winners, its championship points are, for that show, compiled on the basis of which sex had the greater number of points. If there are two points in dogs and four in bitches and the dog goes Best of Winners, then *both* the dog and the

Ch. Orange Park Grover pictured in 1972 winning Best in Show. This son of Ch. Santana-Mandeville's Ichabod ex Ch. Santana-Mandeville's Minnie was bred and owned by Mary B. and R. Milton Meyer, Oranpark Bassets, Orange, California, and enjoyed an important show career under the handling of Jerry and Elaine Rigden.

Ch. Coran Country Cojac, owned by Bert and Mike Salyers and Connie and Randy Fredericksen, shown winning one of his many Groups under judge Mrs. Heywood Hartley. Handled by Jack H. Potts.

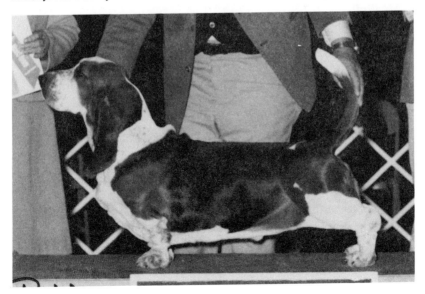

Can. and Am. Ch. Ran-Du's Fancy Farmer, by Ch. Coventry Rock Andy (a son of Ch. Lyn Mar Acres Lord Batoff) ex Orange Park Gidget (daughter of Ch. Orange Park Dexter) at Western Reserve in 1973. A Canadian Best in Show winner, all-breeds. Bred, owned and handled by Mrs. Sue Sutfin, Ran-Su Kennels.

bitch are awarded an equal number of points, in this case four. Should the Winners Dog or the Winners Bitch go on to win Best of Breed or Best of Variety, additional points are accorded for the additional dogs and bitches defeated by so doing, provided, of course, that there were entries specifically for Best of Breed Competition or Specials, as these specific entries are generally called.

If your dog or bitch takes Best of Opposite Sex after going Winners, points are credited according to the number of the same sex defeated in both the regular classes and Specials competition. If Best of Winners is also won, then whatever additional points for each of these awards are available will be credited. Many a one- or two-point win has grown into a major in this manner.

Moving further along, should your dog win its Variety Group from the classes (in other words, if it has taken either Winners Dog or Winners Bitch), you then receive points based on the greatest number of points awarded to any member of any breed included within that Group during that show's competition. Should the day's winning also include Best in Show, the same rule of thumb applies, and your dog or bitch receives the highest number of points awarded to any other dog of any breed at that event.

Best of Breed competition consists of the Winners Dog and the Winners Bitch, who automatically compete on the strength of those awards, in addition to whatever dogs and bitches have been entered specifically for this class for which champions of record are eligible. Since July 1980, dogs who, according to their owner's records, have completed the requirements for a championship after the closing of entries for the show, but whose championships are unconfirmed, may be transferred from one of the regular classes to the Best of Breed competition, provided this transfer is made by the show superintendent or show secretary *prior to the start of any judging at the show.*

This has proved an extremely popular new rule, as under it a dog can finish on Saturday and then be transferred and compete as a Special on Sunday. It must be emphasized that the change *must* be made *prior* to the start of *any* part of the day's judging, not for just your individual breed.

In the United States, Best of Breed winners are entitled to compete in the Variety Group which includes them. This is not mandatory, it is a privilege which exhibitors value. (In Canada, Best of Breed winners *must* compete in the Variety Group, or they lose any points already won.) The dogs winning *first* in each of the seven Variety Groups *must*

De Rorodowade P.K.'s Samantha taking Best of Opposite Sex at Santa Clara Valley for owners Bob and Margaret Reis, Napa, California. Photo courtesy of the Forsyths.

Ch. Coran Captain Jack of MiBerSham, C.D.X., owned by Bert and Mike Salyers and Connie and Randy Fredericksen. Winning a major here handled by Jack H. Potts. Jay is now working towards a U.D. Degree.

compete for Best in Show. Missing the opportunity of taking your dog in for competition in its Group is foolish as it is there where the general public is most likely to notice your breed and become interested in learning about it.

Non-regular classes are sometimes included at the all-breed shows, and they are almost invariably included at Specialty Shows. These include Stud Dog Class and Brood Bitch Class, which are judged on the basis of the quality of the two offspring accompanying the sire or dam. The quality of the latter two is beside the point and should not be considered by the judge; it is the youngsters who count, and the quality of *both* are to be averaged to decide which sire or dam is the best and most consistent producer. Then there is the Brace Class (which, at all-breed shows, moves up to Best Brace in each Variety Group and then Best Brace in Show), which is judged on the similarity and evenness of appearance of the two members of the brace. In other words, the two dogs should look like identical twins in size, color, and conformation and should move together almost as a single dog, one person handling with precision and ease. The same applies to the Team Class competition, except that four dogs are involved and, if necessary, two handlers.

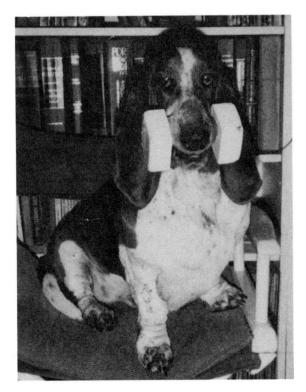

Manor Hill Mona Lisa, C.D.X., in one of her more serious poses. This widely sought after commercial model is owned by Priscilla White, and was bred by the Howard Nygoods. She is by Ch. Pine Patch Bachelor Buttons ex Ch. Manor Hill Baby Tooth.

Ch. Bugle Bay's Bouillon, C.D.X., T.D., ROM, wearing his "tracking suit." Owned by the Cooks, Bugle Bay Bassets, Azle, Texas.

The Veterans Class is for the older dogs, the minimum age of whom is seven years. This class is judged on the quality of the dogs, as the winner competes in Best of Breed competition and has, on a respectable number of occasions, been known to take that top award. So the point is *not* to pick out the oldest dog, as some judges seem to believe, but the best specimen of the breed, exactly as in the regular classes.

Then there are Sweepstakes and Futurity Stakes sponsored by many Specialty clubs, sometimes as part of their regular Specialty Shows and sometimes as separate events on an entirely different occasion. The difference between the two stakes is that Sweepstakes entries usually include dogs from six to eighteen months age with entries made at the same time as the others for the show while for a Futurity the entries are bitches nominated when bred and the individual puppies entered at or shortly following their birth.

If you already show your dog, if you plan on being an exhibitor in the future, or if you simply enjoy attending dog shows, there is a book, which you will find to be an invaluable source of detailed information about all aspects of show dog competition. This book is *Successful Dog Show Exhibiting* (T.F.H. Publications, Inc.) and is available wherever the one you are reading was purchased.

Junior Showmanship Competition

If there is a youngster in your family between the ages of ten and sixteen, there is no better or more rewarding hobby than becoming an active participant in Junior Showmanship. This is a marvelous activity for young people. It teaches responsibility, good sportsmanship, the fun of competition where one's own skills are the deciding factor of success, proper care of a pet, and how to socialize with other young folks. Any youngster may experience the thrill of emerging from the ring a winner and the satisfaction of a good job well done.

Entry in Junior Showmanship Classes is open to any boy or girl who is at least ten years old and under seventeen years old on the day of the show. The Novice Junior Showmanship Class is open to youngsters who have not already won, at the time the entries close, three firsts in this class. Youngsters who have won three firsts in Novice may compete in the Open Junior Showmanship Class. Any junior handler who wins his third first-place award in Novice may participate in the Open Class at the same show, provided that the Open Class has at least one other junior handler entered and competing in it that day. The Novice and Open Classes may be divided into Junior and Senior Classes. Youngsters between the ages of ten and twelve, inclusively, are eligible for the Junior division; and youngsters between thirteen and seventeen, inclusively, are eligible for the Senior division.

Any of the foregoing classes may be separated into individual classes for boys and for girls. If such a division is made, it must be so indicated on the premium list. The premium list also indicates the prize for Best Junior Handler, if such a prize is being offered at the show. Any youngster who wins a first in any of the regular classes may enter the competition for this prize, provided the youngster has been undefeated in any other Junior Showmanship Class at that show.

Junior Showmanship Classes, unlike regular conformation classes in which the quality of the dog is judged, are judged solely on the skill and ability of the junior handling the dog. Which dog is best is not the point—it is which youngster does the best job with the dog that is under consideration. Eligibility requirements for the dog being shown in Junior Showmanship, and other detailed information, can be found in *Regulations for Junior Showmanship*, available from the American Kennel Club.

A junior who has a dog that he or she can enter in both Junior Showmanship and conformation classes has twice the opportunity for success and twice the opportunity to get into the ring and work with the

Best Junior Handler, International Kennel Club of Chicago 1970. Brian Martin, the winner, with Ch. Shadow Hill's Midnight Rodeo. Judge, Roberta Campbell Krohne.

Westminster 1980. Back row, Ed Bivin, Len Brumby, Brian Martin, Peter Martin, and Paul Nigro look on as Heidi Martin, sister of Brian and Peter, makes it fourteen consecutive years that the Martin youngsters have qualified with Top Banana Bassets for competition there.

dog, a combination which can lead to not only awards for expert handling but also, if the dog is of sufficient quality, for making a conformation champion.

Pre-Show Preparations for Your Dog and You

Preparation of the items you will need as a dog show exhibitor should not be left until the last moment. They should be planned and arranged for at least several days in advance of the show in order for you to remain calm and relaxed as the countdown starts.

The importance of the crate has already been mentioned, and we hope it is already part of your equipment. Of equal importance is the grooming table, which very likely you have also already acquired for use at home. You should take it along with you to the shows, as your dog will need last minute touches before entering the ring. Should you have not yet made this purchase, folding tables with rubber tops are made specifically for this purpose and can be purchased at most dog shows, where concession booths with marvelous assortments of "doggy" necessities are to be found, or at your pet supplier. You will also need a sturdy tack box (also available at the dog show concessions) in which to carry your grooming tools and equipment. The latter should include brushes, comb, scissors, nail clippers, whatever you use for last minute clean-up jobs, cotton swabs, first-aid equipment, and anything you are in the habit of using on the dog, including a leash or two of the type you prefer, some well-cooked and dried-out liver or any of the small packaged "dog treats" for use as bait in the ring, an atomizer in case you wish to dampen your dog's coat when you are preparing him for the ring, and so on. A large turkish towel to spread under the dog on the grooming table is also useful.

Take a large thermos or cooler of ice, the biggest one you can accommodate in your vehicle, for use by "man and beast." Take a jug of water (there are lightweight, inexpensive ones available at all sporting goods shops) and a water dish. If you plan to feed the dog at the show, or if you and the dog will be away from home more than one day, bring food for him from home so that he will have the type to which he is accustomed.

You may or may not have an exercise pen. It is a *must*, even if you only have one dog. While the shows do provide areas for the exercise of the dogs, these are among the most likely places to have your dog come in contact with any illnesses which may be going around, and having a pen of your own for your dog's use is excellent protection.

Such a pen can be used in other ways, too, such as a place other than the crate in which to put the dog to relax (that is roomier than the crate) and a place in which the dog can exercise at motels and rest areas. These, too, are available at the show concession stands and come in a variety of heights and sizes. A set of "pooper scoopers" should also be part of your equipment, along with a package of plastic bags for cleaning up after your dog.

Bring along folding chairs for the members of your party, unless all of you are fond of standing, as these are almost never provided anymore by the clubs. Have your name stamped on the chairs so that there will be no doubt as to whom the chairs belong. Bring whatever you and your family enjoy for drinks or snacks in a picnic basket or cooler, as show food, in general, is expensive and usually not great. You should always have a pair of boots, a raincoat, and a rain hat with

A picture filled with Basset nostalgia and history! In 1966, British judge Douglas Appleton awarding Best of Breed to Ch. Santana-Mandeville Rodney, Bobby Barlow handling for owner Leonard Skolnick, on the left. Best of Winners to Rodney's son, Keithann Winnie the Pooh, owned by Keith Haygood, on the right.

you (they should remain permanently in your vehicle if you plan to attend shows regularly), as well as a sweater, a warm coat, and a change of shoes. A smock or big cover-up apron will assure that you remain tidy as you prepare the dog for the ring. Your overnight case should include a small sewing kit for emergency repairs, bandaids, headache and indigestion remedies, and any personal products or medications you normally use.

In your car you should always carry maps of the area where you are headed and an assortment of motel directories. Generally speaking, we have found Holiday Inns to be the nicest about taking dogs. Ramadas and Howard Johnsons generally do as cheerfully (with a few exceptions). Best Western generally frowns on pets (not always, but often enough to make it necessary to find out which do). Some of the smaller chains welcome pets. The majority of privately owned motels do not.

Have everything prepared the night before the show to expedite your departure. Be sure that the dog's identification and your judging program and other show information are in your purse or briefcase. If you are taking sandwiches, have them ready. Anything that goes into the car the night before the show will be one thing less to remember in the morning. Decide upon what you will wear and have it out and ready. If there is any question in your mind about what to wear, try on the possibilities before the day of the show; don't risk feeling you may want to change when you see yourself dressed a few moments prior to departure time!

In planning your outfit, make it something simple that will not detract from your dog. Remember that a dark dog silhouettes attractively against a light background and vice-versa. Sport clothes always seem to look best at dog shows, preferably conservative in type and not overly "loud" as you do not want to detract from your dog, who should be the focus of interest at this point. What you wear on your feet is important. Many types of flooring can be hazardously slippery, as can wet grass. Make it a habit to wear rubber soles and low or flat heels in the ring for your own safety, especially if you are showing a dog that likes to move out smartly.

Your final step in pre-show preparation is to leave yourself plenty of time to reach the show that morning. Traffic can get amazingly heavy as one nears the immediate area of the show, finding a parking place can be difficult, and other delays may occur. You'll be in better humor to enjoy the day if your trip to the show is not fraught with panic over fear of not arriving in time!

Enjoying the Dog Show

From the moment of your arrival at the show until after your dog has been judged, keep foremost in your mind the fact the he is your reason for being there and that he should therefore be the center of your attention. Arrive early enough to have time for those last-minute touches that can make such a great difference when he enters the ring. Be sure that he has ample time to exercise and that he attends to personal matters. A dog arriving in the ring and immediately using it as an exercise pen hardly makes a favorable impression on the judge.

When you reach ringside, ask the steward for your arm-card and anchor it firmly into place on your arm. Make sure that you are where you should be when your class is called. The fact that you have picked up your arm-card does not guarantee, as some seem to think, that the judge will wait for you. The judge has a full schedule which he wishes to complete on time. Even though you may be nervous, assume an air of calm self-confidence. Remember that this is a hobby to be enjoyed, so approach it in that state of mind. The dog will do better, too, as he will be quick to reflect your attitude.

Always show your dog with an air of pride. If you make mistakes in presenting him, don't worry about it. Next time you will do better. Do not permit the presence of more experienced exhibitors to intimidate you. After all, they, too, once were newcomers.

The judging routine usually starts when the judge asks that the dogs be gaited in a circle around the ring. During this period the judge is watching each dog as it moves, noting style, topline, reach and drive, head and tail carriage, and general balance. Keep your mind and your eye on your dog, moving him at his most becoming gait and keeping your place in line without coming too close to the exhibitor ahead of you. Always keep your dog on the inside of the circle, between yourself and the judge, so that the judge's view of the dog is unobstructed.

Calmly pose the dog when requested to set up for examination. If you are at the head of the line and many dogs are in the class, go all the way to the end of the ring before starting to stack the dog, leaving sufficient space for those behind you to line theirs up as well as requested by the judge. If you are not at the head of the line but between other exhibitors, leave sufficient space ahead of your dog for the judge to examine him. The dogs should be spaced so that the judge is able to move among them to see them from all angles. In practicing to "set up" or "stack" your dog for the judge's examination, bear in mind the importance of doing so quickly and with dexterity. The judge has a

Ch. Seifenjagenheim Domino, by Ch. Lyn Mar's Clown ex Ch. Webb's Blac Amanda from their second breeding. Owned by Mrs. Queenie Wickstrom, handled by Dorothy Hardy. Cy Rickel is the judge (left), Mrs. Sara Peterman looking on. From the collection of the late Frank and Dorothy Hardy.

Ch. Jeffrey Joker taking Best American-bred in Show at Mid-Hudson in 1961.

Fort Merrill Lieutenant, by Strathalbyn Sidhiron ex Strathalbyn Bethsheba, has almost completed title as we go to press. Born September 1981, bred by Joan Urban, owned by C.R. Fredericksen and Bert and Mike Salyers.

Helen Smith with her beautiful and highly successful winning bitch of the late 1960's, Ch. Helwal's Catherine The Great, taking Best of Breed from Anna Katherine Nicholas, judge. Helen and Walter Smith produced many handsome Bassets at their Helwal Kennels in New Jersey, later located in the Carolinas.

Ch. Coran Col Gauss of Mibersham is owned by Bert & Mike Salyers and Connie & Randy Fredericksen. He finished his Championship under judge Marcia Foy June 25, 1978, handled to his title by Jack H. Potts. Shown with co-owner Randy Fredericksen.

schedule to meet and only a few moments in which to evaluate each dog. You will immeasurably help yours to make a favorable impression if you are able to "get it all together" in a minimum amount of time. Practice at home before a mirror can be a great help toward bringing this about, facing the dog so that you see him from the same side that the judge will and working to make him look right in the shortest length of time.

240

Listen carefully as the judge describes the manner in which the dog is to be gaited, whether it is straight down and straight back; down the ring, across, and back; or in a triangle. The latter has become the most popular pattern with the majority of judges. "In a triangle" means the dog should move down the outer side of the ring to the first corner, across that end of the ring to the second corner, and then back to the judge from the second corner, using the center of the ring in a diagonal line. Please learn to do this pattern without breaking at each corner to twirl the dog around you, a senseless maneuver we sometimes have noted. Judges like to see the dog in an uninterrupted triangle, as they are thus able to get a better idea of the dog's gait.

It is impossible to overemphasize that the gait at which you move your dog is tremendously important, and considerable study and thought should be given to the matter. At home, have someone move the dog for you at different speeds so that you can tell which shows him off to best advantage. The most becoming action almost invariably is seen at a moderate gait, head up and topline holding. Do not gallop your dog around the ring or hurry him into a speed atypical of his breed. Nothing being rushed appears at its best; give your dog a chance to move along at his (and the breed's) natural gait. For a dog's action to be judged accurately, that dog should move with strength and power but not excessive speed, holding a straight line as he goes to and from the judge.

As you bring the dog back to the judge, stop him a few feet away and be sure that he is standing in a becoming position. Bait him to show the judge an alert expression, using whatever tasty morsel he has been trained to expect for this purpose or, if that works better for you, use a small squeak-toy in your hand. A reminder, please, to those using liver or treats. Take them with you when you leave the ring. Do not just drop them on the ground where they will be found by another dog.

When the awards have been made, accept yours graciously, no matter how you actually may feel about it. What's done is done, and arguing with a judge or stomping out of the ring is useless and a reflection on your sportsmanship. Be courteous, congratulate the winner if your dog was defeated, and try not to show your disappointment. By the same token, please be a gracious winner; this, surprisingly, sometimes seems to be still more difficult.

Ch. Placid Farm's King Solemn-Un, C.D., sitting up tall to receive his ribbon. Owned by Jacqueline Adams, Newtown, Conn. and LaVerne Anderson, Bryant, Arkansas.

Chapter 12

Your Basset and Obedience

For its own protection and safety, every dog should be taught, at the very least, to recognize and obey the commands "Come," "Heel," "Down," "Sit," and "Stay." Doing so at some time might save the dog's life and in less extreme circumstances will certainly make him a better behaved, more pleasant member of society. If you are patient and enjoy working with your dog, study some of the excellent books available on the subject of obedience and then teach your canine friend these basic manners. If you need the stimulus of working with a group, find out where obedience training classes are held (usually your veterinarian, your dog's breeder, or a dog-owning friend can tell you) and you and your dog can join up. Alternatively, you could let someone else do the training by sending the dog to class, but this is not very rewarding because you lose the opportunity of working with your dog and the pleasure of the rapport thus established.

If you are going to do it yourself, there are some basic rules which you should follow. You must remain calm and confident in attitude. Never lose your temper and frighten or punish your dog unjustly. Be quick and lavish with praise each time a command is correctly followed. Make it fun for the dog and he will be eager to please you by responding correctly. Repetition is the keynote, but it should not be continued without recess to the point of tedium. Limit the training sessions to ten- or fifteen-minute periods at a time.

Formal obedience training can be followed, and very frequently is, by entering the dog in obedience competition to work toward an obedience degree, or several of them, depending on the dog's aptitude and your own enjoyment. Obedience trials are held in conjunction with the majority of all-breed conformation dog shows, with Specialty

Brownridge Bootlegger, C.D., T.D.X., Can. T.D.X., Bda. T.D., is the first Basset to have gained a T.D.X. title in the United States. Susan A. and Thomas C. Boyd, owners, St. Louis, Missouri.

shows, and frequently as separate Specialty events. If you are working alone with your dog, a list of trial dates might be obtained from your dog's veterinarian, your dog breeder, or a dog-owning friend; the A.K.C. *Gazette* lists shows and trials to be scheduled in the coming months; and if you are a member of a training class, you will find the information readily available.

The goals for which one works in the formal A.K.C. Member or Licensed Trials are the following titles: Companion Dog (C.D.), Companion Dog Excellent (C.D.X.), and Utility Dog (U.D.). These degrees are earned by receiving three "legs," or qualifying scores, at each level of competition. The degrees must be earned in order, with one completed prior to starting work on the next. For example, a dog must have earned C.D. prior to starting work on C.D.X.; then C.D.X. must be completed before U.D. work begins. The ultimate title attainable in obedience work is Obedience Trial Champion (O.T.Ch.).

When you see the letters "C.D." following a dog's name, you will know that this dog has satisfactorily completed the following exercises: heel on leash, heel free, stand for examination, recall, long sit and long stay. "C.D.X." means that tests have been passed on all of those just mentioned plus heel free, drop on recall, retrieve over high jump, broad jump, long sit, and long down. "U.D." indicates that the

Ch. Winnward Brandywine, U.D.T.X. The breed's first Champion U.D.T. and the breed's first Champion U.D.T.X. Brandywine earned his U.D. March 22nd 1981, his T.D.X. Degree February 28th 1982. Bred by Margaret Pearce and Betty Jean Jones. Owned by J.C. and K.J. Green, Littleton, Colorado.

dog has additionally passed tests in scent discrimination (leather article), scent discrimination (metal article), signal exercises, directed retrieve, directed jumping, and group stand for examination. The letters "O.T.Ch." are the abbreviation for the only obedience title which precedes rather than follows a dog's name. To gain an obedience trial championship, a dog who already holds a Utility Dog degree must win a total of one hundred points and must win three firsts, under three different judges, in Utility and Open B Classes.

There is also a Tracking Dog title (T.D.) which can be earned at tracking trials. In order to pass the tracking tests the dog must follow the trail of a stranger along a path on which the trail was laid between thirty minutes and two hours previously. Along this track there must be more than two right-angle turns, at least two of which are well out in the open where no fences or other boundaries exist for the guidance of the dog or the handler. The dog wears a harness and is connected to the handler by a lead twenty to forty feet in length. Inconspicuously dropped at the end of the track is an article to be retrieved, usually a glove or wallet, which the dog is expected to locate and the handler to pick up. The letters "T.D.X." are the abbreviation for Tracking Dog Excellent, a more difficult version of the Tracking Dog test with a longer track and more turns to be worked through.

The First Obedience Trial
Champion Basset Hound

It was Obedience Trial Champion Buzz Taylor's Goober, T.D., who distinguished himself by attaining the honor of becoming the first obedience trial champion Basset Hound. Goober completed his championship in just seven months. This included two High in Trials, eight first prizes, and four second places which amounted to 105 obedience trial championship points. Goober is the first Basset Hound in the United States to earn this title and is the third dog of any breed in his home state of Florida to have achieved the accomplishment. He is the second obedience trial champion for owner-handler-trainer Buzz Taylor, who earlier had completed the first obedience trial champion from Florida, a Labrador Retriever named Tar.

Lena Wray with five of her tracking dogs. *Left* to *right*, Ch. Party Doll's Geraldine, T.D.; Slippery Hill Bonnie Parker, T.D. (pointed); Earnest's Shirley Black Kettle, T.F.; Ch. Julie of Rockin-Pas, T.D.; and Ch. Bret Mavrik of Rockin-Pas, T.D. The Wrays live at Jupiter, Florida.

Goober is from the third generation of Buzz Taylor's nationally famed obedience Bassets. Many fanciers will recall Bridlespur Nudger, U.D., and Santana's Briget, U.D., who were the Number One and Number Two obedience-rated Bassets of the 1960's. These were Goober's grandparents. His dam, Buzz Taylor's Autumn, U.D.T., and his uncle, Buzz Taylor's Hopalong, U.D.T., both were top-rated and thrilled many a crowd of spectators as they won and placed at important obedience trials, including the U.S. Obedience Classics and the Basset Hound Club of America Specialties.

Goober was sired by Champion Laverne's Golden Boy. His grandfather was Champion . Laverne's Launcelot Gobbo. His great-grandsire was the famous Sir Tomo of Glenhaven.

Goober retired in 1983 at eight years of age. Now he assists Mr. Taylor by acting as "demonstration dog" at his clinics. Also, if Mr. Taylor ever can find the time away from his busy schedule of judging and exhibiting, he would still like to have Goober acquire his T.D.X. since Goober's parents were trackers.

Goober's talents did not just happen; they were bred into him by a very carefully thought out and selective program. His dam, Buzz Taylor's Autumn, U.D.T., gained records equal to his own, except that she was a bit too early for the obedience trial championship which was not created until shortly after her day. At the first Gaines Classic, in Chicago, however, she placed seventh in the Super Dog Class. The dogs behind Goober were famed show winners of the past; and brains, speed, and ability all were there. To quote Mr. Taylor, "Believe me, planned breeding *does* prove worthwhile."

A bright, intelligent bitch, Minerva Moose Mouse, was bred to Goober, as a result producing a beautiful daughter whom Mr. Taylor feels will be his next obedience star. She is Buzz Taylor's Zibbilean and shows great promise of following in her distinguished sire's pawprints.

Mr. Taylor has proven a point in achieving the success that he has with Goober and his earlier Bassets, for many people are inclined to disbelieve that Bassets can succeed in this field. Very definitely they *can* and *do* if trained and handled properly. Goober is a shining example of that fact, which we hope will be emphasized still further by Zibbilean! Goober has qualified at every Classic in which he has competed; and even though he did not win or place, his qualifying to be in there, his being welcomed and admired, and his competing with the best dogs in the country meant a great deal to Goober, his handler, and to the breed. Goober is a credit to Bassets. We salute him sincerely!

BeeLee's Pruneface Prudence was the second U.D.T. Basset in the United States, back in 1964. Owned by Lena and Billy Wray of Jupiter, Florida. The first Utility Dog Tracker in 1963, Pierre Bonne Joie, was owned by Benjamin Harris, Encino, California.

248

This is Pierre's Bonne Joie, U.D.T., who came out of a 5-year retirement at the age of eight to be the first Basset Hound of record to receive a Utility Dog Tracker degree. She was the third Basset to receive a U.D. Joie gained her U.D.T. degree in 1963. Owner, Benjamin I. Harris, Encino, California.

Ch. Strathalbyn Shoot To Kill, C.D., T.D., No. 1 conformation Basset Hound in the U.S. in 1979, has 136 Best of Breed wins, 18 Hound Group firsts, and 50 Hound Group placements. The only Top Winning Basset to have earned obedience and tracking titles, Michael is the first member of a registered Hound pack to have won a Best in Show. Kay and Craig Green, owners. Eric F. George, breeder.

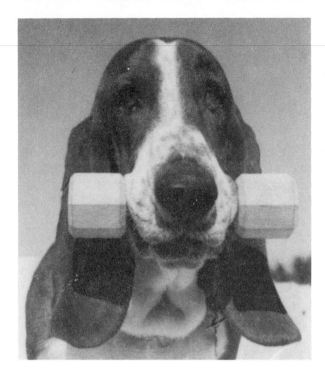

T.D.X. Basset Hounds as of May 1984

Only seven Bassets to date have acquired the very prestigious title of Tracking Dog Excellent (T.D.X.) as this book goes to press. A complete list of them follows, in the order in which their titles were completed:

1) Brownridge Bootlegger, C.D., T.D.X., Can. T.D.X., Bda. T.D. —Owned by Susan A. and Thomas Boyd.

2) Governor M. McDuffy, C.D.X., T.D.X.—Owned by Sally B. Davis.

3) Bee Lee's Tracking Schooze, C.D., T.D.X.—Owned by Sally J. Elkins.

4) Ch. Winnwars Brandywine, U.D.T.X.—Owned by Kathryn J. Green.

5) Dig 'Em Widetrack, C.D., T.D.X.—Owned by Joyce A. Capoccia.

6) Arrowstone Earth Angel Clara, T.D.X.—Owned by Linda and Herbert E. Brown.

7). Gerianne's Esther Marie, U.D.T.X.—Owned by Gerianne F. and George W. Darnell.

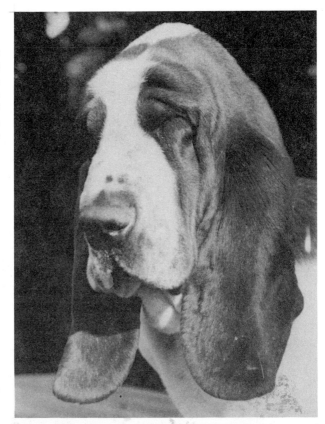

A lovely head study of Ch. Jacquart's Buffalo Bill, C.D. bred by Jennifer L. Jacquart, owned by Kay Green, Littleton, Colorado.

Jagersven Bluejay, T.D., owned by Lena Wray, Jupiter, Florida.

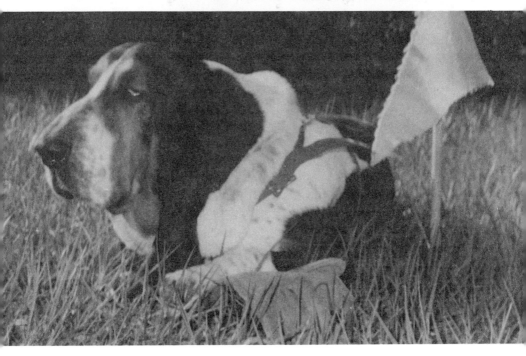

Field Ch. Deepgrass Oliver Wendell, courtesy of Dr. and Mrs. Leonard Skolnick.

Chapter 13

Bassets in the Field

Bassets are an excellent breed with which to work in the field, whether you are interested in doing so informally just for the pleasure of it or, more seriously, in taking your dog through formal field trials to a degree. Depending on your inclinations, you can have fun either way, as the Basset's heredity makes him seem to know instinctively what is expected of him and how to go about it. Of course, training is needed to direct these tendencies into the right channels; but you will be surprised how quickly your Basset will learn and how capable in his work he may become.

Bassets are scent hounds, working entirely with their noses. The Basset does not catch the rabbit and he does not chase it. Rather, he works it along to where the hunter awaits, slowly and steadily edging it nearer as the hunter watches and positions himself to take it.

In field trial competition, hunting is forbidden. Here the "hunter" is concerned with and takes his pleasure in seeing how the Basset trails the rabbit. The rabbits are unharmed as it is necessary to keep up the population if the grounds are to remain stocked for future trials.

At the field trials, competition is divided as follows: Derbies, All Age Dogs, All Age Bitches, and Champion Stakes. The Derby and Champion Classes are considered to be Non-regular, and the winners are not awarded points toward a field trial championship. Bassets under two years of age are eligible for Derby Classes; thus they are really try-out competitions for the youngsters.

To become a field champion, a Basset must place in Open All Age Classes at no less than four trials, have at least once placed first, and have won a total of 60 championship points. The points are awarded as follows, based on the number of "starters:" To the winner of first

Basset Dog Stake, Basset Hound Club of America Nationals 1981. Photo courtesy of Leonard and Marge Skolnick.

place, one point for each competitor awarded to the winner; to the second place winner, a half point for each competitor; for the third place winner, a quarter of a point for each competitor; for fourth place, an eighth of a point for each competitor. After this comes the "next Best Qualified Hound," or N.B.Q. This dog does not receive either points or a placement and does *not* get moved up even should a disqualification of any of the placed hounds take place.

The title "Grand Champion" has recently been created, awarded by the Basset Hound Club of America to Bassets winning a total of twenty points from the Field Champion Class. These are awarded on the basis of four points for first place, three points for second place, two points for third place, and one point for fourth.

The title "Dual Champion" is bestowed upon Bassets who have fulfilled *both* the American Kennel Club requirements for a field championship and a bench championship. To this date, May 20th 1984, only the following Bassets have earned this honor:

1) Kazoo's Moses the Great—By Champion Casey of Kazoo ex Champion Long View Acres Donna. Dog. Bred by Mary Jo Shields. Owned by Jim Dohr. 1964.

2) Helwal's Desire—By Champion Lyn-Mar Acres Barrister ex Helwal's Hooligan. Bitch. Bred by Walter and Helen Smith. 1969.

3) Braun's Wholly Thursday—By Champion Trojan Echo's Erebus ex Braun's Apjo Mini. Bitch. Bred by J.M. and A.I. Hutchinson. Owned by A. Braun.

4) Daisy's Dopey—By Dunn's Rusty Dusty Asa ex Barker's Daisy Belle. Dog. Bred by M.E. Dunn. Owned by W.J. Luce. 1971.

5) Double B's Lucky Libertine—By Champion Hubertus Playboy ex Champion Double B's Veronica. Dog. Bred by Helen Boutell. Owned by R. and L. Wells. 1972.

6) Slippery Hill Cinnamon, C.D.—By Champion Santana-Mande-ville Egghead ex Slippery Hill Felice. Bitch. Bred by D. Barnes. Owned by Leonard Skolnick. 1975.

7) Pettit's Ranger Ric—By Field Champion Rosie's Jeff ex Field Champion Dohrshire's Twiggy. Dog. Bred and owned by T. and S. Pettit. 1977.

8) Jackson's Samantha Lu—By Meadow Beauty Lucky ex Pinehill's Greta Lynn. Bitch. Bred by J.M. Foster. Owned by S. Ellingwood. 1977.

Champion and Field Trial Champion Branscombe's Man of La Mancha, T.D., who has just become the third Basset in history to hold a dual championship plus a third title, owned and trained by Branscombe Bassets, Francis and Ruth Paule, Riverton, Illinois.

The First Dual Champion Basset Hound *Bitch*, Ch. Helwal's Desire, by Ch. Lyn-Mar Acres Barrister ex Helwal's Hooligan, bred and owned by Helen and Walter Smith, Helwal Bassets. Desire finished her show championship and then her field championship with a two year lapse (1966-1968) in between, the result of a temporary forced retirement when she was struck by a car while out hunting. For awhile there were doubts whether she would ever walk again, but in 1969 she finished for her dual!

Field Champion Slippery Hill Yours Truly, Field Trial Basset of the Year 1979. Owned by Dr. and Mrs. Leonard Skolnick.

Brace of Bassets on the trail of the rabbit. Photo by Sally Foster.

Putting dog on the line in a field trial. Photo courtesy of Dr. and Mrs. Leonard Skolnick.

The first ten Grand Field Champion Bassets were:

1) Hamlin's Dolly—By Field Champion Hamlin's Torpedo ex Field Champion Irle's Cleopatra.

2) McWilliam's Dixie Belle, by McWilliam's Buccaneer ex McWilliam's Dixie Peach.

3) Van's Fantasy, by Field Champion Beacon Tick Tock ex Crelin's Lady Fair.

4) Tagg About's Pluto, by Sandy Hill Homer ex Field Champion Tagg About's Porsche.

5) Slippery Hill Sophie, by Field Champion Slippery Hill Calvin ex Field Champion Beldean's Slippery Hill Sam.

6) Sykemoor Nestor, by Dalewell Rambler ex Sykemoor Jaya.

7) Mickey's At Last, by Azul Rayo ex Crelin's Fancy Dancer.

8) Tagg About's Jensen, by Field Champion Tagg About Pluto ex Brookline's Minn.

9) Campbell's Rebel Queen, by Field Champion Rosie's Bill ex Campbell's Cindy Lou.

10) Slippery Hill Stub, by Field Champion Slippery Hill Calvin ex Field Champion Beldean's Slippery Hill Sam.

Those wishing complete information on the subject should contact the American Kennel Club (51 Madison Avenue, New York NY 10010) and request a copy of their free booklet, *Basset Hound Field Trial Rules and Standard Procedures*. The Basset Hound Club of America also has a most comprehensive and informative booklet on the subject of Bassets in the field, *Field Training with a Basset Hound*, which should be available (for a small charge) to interested parties. The address of the current secretary of the Basset Hound Club of America is also available from the American Kennel Club.

It is the general feeling that puppies should not be started on field work earlier than six months of age. This, however, does not mean that basic obedience training should be deferred that length of time. The earlier your pup learns such useful points as the meaning of "sit," "down," "come," "stay," and so on, the better off both you and he will be, as this basic training is very helpful when you start to turn your puppy loose in the field.

Exciting and eventful news just as we go to press—Field Champion Branscombe's Man of La Mancha just completed his bench championship, thus becoming only the third Basset in history to hold a dual championship plus a third title. This dog attained all three within the period of one year. His grandsire, Branscombe Troilus, was the second Basset to score this combination of titles. Slippery Hill Hudson was the first.

A special note on Mancha. This dog sustained an early leg injury requiring surgery to prevent an arthritic joint. As a result he was held back from any serious activity until he was eighteen months old, and then he was started on rabbit, partly to help him forget about a "habit limp." As he approached three years of age, he had apparently matured, for between September 1983 and the end of May 1984, he earned 70 field trial points with three first placements and three seconds, the eleven show points he still needed (including a five-point major), and twice qualified in tracking—a comment on that difficult task of waiting until a dog is ready! Mancha has been entirely trained and handled by his owners, Francis and Ruth Paule.

The Coldstream Pack winning at the Bryn Mawr Hound Show.

260

Chapter 14

Hound Shows and American Basset Packs

Hound shows are prestigious competitions both in the United States and in Great Britain. The Peterborough in England, the Clonmel in Ireland, and Bryn Mawr in the United States are all quite rightly looked upon with tremendous respect.

These hound shows are not held under the jurisdiction of the kennel clubs which control bench show activities. They come under the auspices of the Association of the Master of Harriers and Beagles in Britain, the Association of Irish Masters in Ireland, and the National Beagle Club in the United States. These groups maintain their own Stud Books, handling registration of the recognized packs, and it is they that cover the hound shows in each of their countries.

Hound shows provide classification for single hounds, couples and two couples, four couples, and eight couples. Individual conformation is evaluated on the same standard as at bench shows, with the same size limits effective. Packs are judged on the evenness of type and similarity of the hounds, the control with which they are presented, and the correctness of the livery of the hunt servants. Never feel that just any group of Bassets makes a pack. This is definitely not true. Careful work, selection, and training go into assembling one; and each pack member must cooperate, obey commands, and work smoothly with the others. Similarity of appearance is necessary if the pack is to be uniform.

The method of judging at hound shows differs between Great Britain and the United States. In Britain the dogs are brought into the ring

Joint Meet in 1982 of Timber Ridge Bassets and Ashland Bassets at Waterford, Virginia. Edward Copsey, Hon. Sec'y and Whipper-in. Meena Rogers, Master and Huntsman for Timber Ridge. Alen Olson, Huntsman for Ashland. Photo by Richard Lilley.

on leash; then the leads are removed and the judge's evaluations made as the hounds move freely around the enclosed area. In America the hounds are kept on the lead and individually handled by the judge, much in the same manner as at bench shows.

Bryn Mawr, held at the beginning of June each year in Eastern Pennsylvania is an exciting spectacle. The breeds included are Bassets, Beagles, Fox Hounds, and Harriers and it is an event to be thoroughly enjoyed by all who love these breeds.

There are currently ten active, recognized Basset packs in the United States. Only three of these are composed totally of purebred A.K.C.-registered Bassets. Two A.K.C.-registered packs are pending recognition, and there are two A.K.C. registered outlaw packs (not recognized by the National Beagle Club). The following list, given in chronological order by date of recognition, was compiled for us by Meena Rogers to whom we are most grateful. The masters of these packs I am sure are most willing to help newcomers wishing to form their own packs and acquiring suitable hounds for this purpose at moderate prices.

Bryn Mawr Hound Show, June 1966. Champion Basset Hound, Champion Coldstream Charlie Brown with Joe McKenna, M B H. Meena Rogers, judge.

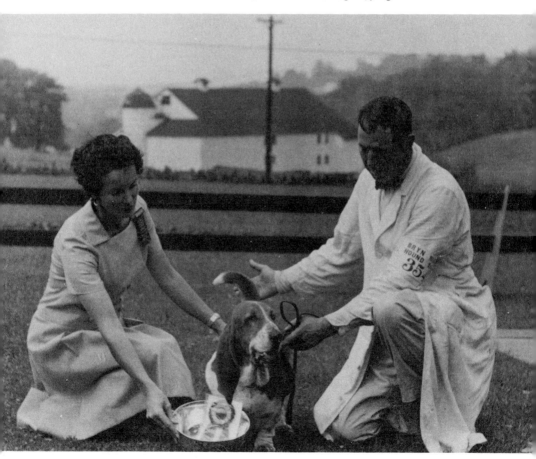

TIMBER RIDGE BASSETS, 4673 Black Rock Road, Hampstead, MD 21074—Purebred A.K.C.-registered. Recognized in 1947. Amelia F. Rogers, Master.

SKYCASTLE FRENCH HOUNDS, Chester Springs, PA 19425—Purebred French and English Basset/Harrier cross. Recognized in 1952. Elizabeth Streeter, Master.

TEWKSBURY FOOT BASSETS, Far Hills, NJ 07931—English Basset/Harrier cross. Recognized in 1953. Masters: James S. Jones, Joseph B. Wiley, Jr., and John P. Ike, III.

ASHLAND BASSETS, Elway Hall, Warrenton, VA 22186—Purebred A.K.C.-registered. Recognized in 1961. Masters: Mrs. Harcourt Lees and Mrs. James J. Wilson.

Timber Ridge entry, Campbell's Lazy Liz, Reserve Champion Bitch Bryn Mawr 1981. Champion A.K.C. Basset and Champion Bitch, Bryn Mawr 1983. By Ch. Tal-E-Ho's Jet, C.D.X. ex Ch. Brendan's Vanessa. Gayle Bontecou, judge. Meena **Rogers**, handling.

Ch. Butz's Yankee Boy, owned by Leslie Kelly, Belbay Kennels, New Alexandria, Pa., won Entered Dog at Bryn Mawr Hound Show in 1980.

THREE CREEK BASSETS (formerly Strathalbyn Bassets), 71 Wolfram Road, St. Charles, MO 63301—Purebred A.K.C.-registered and English/Harrier cross. Recognized in 1966. Masters: Mrs. Walter L. Moore, Laura M. Carpenter, and Dustin H. Griffin.

WINWARD BASSET HOUNDS, Mile Creek Road, Old Lyme, CT 06371—Purebred A.K.C.-registered and English/Harrier cross. Recognized in 1971. C. Bickford Henchey, Master.

SPRING CREEK BASSETS, Barrington, IL 60010—English Basset/Harrier cross. Recognized in 1973. Masters: Frank D. Kenney, Stephen C. Flint, Mrs. Diana Flint, and Mrs. Virginia B. Kenney.

WAYNE DUPAGE FOOT BASSETS, Wayne, IN 60184—Purebred A.K.C.-registered. Recognized in 1973. Masters: Dr. Betsy Kjellstrom and Dr. Ted Kjellstrom.

Timber Ridge entry, Upland Countess, at Bryn Mawr Hound Show 1955, where she was Champion Basset Bitch. Meena Rogers handling. Countess was bought from Mrs. Porter in 1950 by the Hon. Philip K. Crowe (Kingsland Beagles), Easton, Maryland, and kindly given to the Rogers by this gentleman, who also gave them his hunt colors, old gold with infantry blue piping.

Am. and Can. Ch. Strathalbyn Panic at seven months. Handled by Bill Busch; owned by Strathalbyn, Mr. and Mrs. Eric F. George.

SANDANONA HARE HOUNDS, Millbrook, NY 12545—English Basset/Harrier cross. Recognized in 1977. Masters: Oakleigh B. Thorne and Mrs. James M. Park.

BONNIWELL BASSET HOUNDS, Mequon, WI 53092—English Basset/Harrier cross. Recognized in 1982. Mrs. Paul Gladstone, Master.

THE WEYMOUTH BASSETS, Box 86, Southern Pines, NC 28387 (Pending recognition)—Purebred A.K.C.-registered. Organized in 1983. Mrs. Joan C. Thiele, Master.

MARLBOROUGH BASSETS, 15 Marlborough Road, Newtown Square, PA 19073 (Pending recognition)—Purebred A.K.C.-registered. Organized in 1983. Jane Mangram Casserley, Master.

STRATHALBYN BASSET HOUNDS, Crescent, MO 63018 (Outlaw pack)—Purebred A.K.C.-registered. Organized in 1979. Masters: Mr. Eric F. George and Erica V. George, M.D.

MRS. COCHRAN'S HOUNDS, Glyndon, MD 21071 (Outlaw pack)—Purebred A.K.C.-registered. Organized in 1983. Mrs. Peyton S. Cochran, Master.

It is interesting to note that the Tewksbury Foot Bassets and the Skycastle Bassets started with purebred A.K.C. hounds. Jimmy Jones and the Tewksbury went over to an English Basset/Harrier cross; Elizabeth Streeter and her Skycastle went to a pure Griffon-Vendeen and then crossed with the English Basset/Harrier cross.

The English Harrier cross made a much faster pack, hunting more on the order of a pack of Beagles. The French cross has a terrier quality—very busy, fast, and excellent and aggressive in heavy cover. The purebred Basset is slower (but certainly fast enough to leave you gasping for breath), very steady, and true in the open and overgrown fields and woods; and they are not as anxious to go into dense cover, probably because of their great size, although most bitches will ram their way into the densest thickets.

All three types of Basset packs have their good and bad points. In the final analysis, it is a matter of preference—how energetic you want to be, what age you are, whether you want to ride to hounds or want to watch hounds work in a leisurely fashion. What it adds up to is this: The type of hunting that appeals to you, and affords pleasure and excitement, is the right one for you.

This gorgeous headstudy is of Ch. Joan Urban's Honey West, by Ch. Nancy Evans Sir Galahad ex Champion Sisus Chere Amie, belonging to Joan Urban of Dinero, Texas.

Chapter 15

Breeding Your Basset

The Basset Brood Bitch

We have in an earlier chapter discussed selection of a bitch you plan to use for breeding. In making this important purchase, you will be choosing a bitch who you hope will become the foundation of your kennel. Thus she must be of the finest producing bloodlines, excellent in temperament, of good type, and free of major faults or unsoundness. If you are offered a "bargain" brood bitch, be wary, as for this purchase you should not settle for less than the best and the price will be in accordance with the quality.

Conscientious breeders feel quite strongly that the only possible reason for producing puppies is the ambition to improve and uphold quality and temperament within the breed—definitely *not* because one hopes to make a quick cash profit on a mediocre litter, which never seems to work out that way in the long run and which accomplishes little beyond perhaps adding to the nation's heartbreaking number of unwanted canines. The only reason ever for breeding a litter is, with conscientious people, a desire to improve the quality of dogs in their own kennel or, as pet owners, because they wish to add to the number of dogs they themselves own with a puppy or two from their present favorites. In either case breeding should not take place unless one has definitely prospective owners for as many puppies as the litter may contain, lest you find yourself with several fast-growing young dogs and no homes in which to place them.

Bitches should not be mated earlier than their second season, by which time they should be from fifteen to eighteen months old. Many breeders prefer to wait and first finish the championships of their show bitches before breeding them, as pregnancy can be a disaster to a show coat and getting the bitch back in shape again takes time. When you have decided what will be the proper time, start watching at least several months ahead for what you feel would be the perfect mate to best complement your bitch's quality and bloodlines. Subscribe to the magazines which feature your breed exclusively and to some which cover all breeds in order to familiarize yourself with outstanding stud dogs in areas other than your own for there is no necessity nowadays to limit your choice to a nearby dog unless you truly like him and feel that he is the most suitable. It is quite usual to ship a bitch to a stud dog a distance away, and this generally works out with no ill effects. The important thing is that you need a stud dog strong in those features where your bitch is weak or lacking and of bloodlines compatible to hers. Compare the background of both your bitch and the stud dog under consideration, paying particular attention to the quality of the puppies from bitches with backgrounds similar to your bitch's. If the puppies have been of the type and quality you admire, then this dog would seem a sensible choice for yours, too.

Stud fees may be a few hundred dollars, sometimes even more under special situations for a particularly successful sire. It is money well spent, however. Do *not* ever breed to a dog because he is less expensive than the others unless you honestly believe that he can sire the kind of puppies who will be a credit to your kennel and your breed.

Contacting the owners of the stud dogs you find interesting will bring you pedigrees and pictures which you can then study in relation to your bitch's pedigree and conformation. Discuss your plans with other breeders who are knowledgeable (including the one who bred your own bitch). You may not always receive an entirely unbiased opinion (particularly if the person giving it also has an available stud dog), but one learns by discussion so listen to what they say, consider their opinions, and then you may be better qualified to form your own opinion.

As soon as you have made a choice, phone the owner of the stud dog you wish to use to find out if this will be agreeable. You will be asked about the bitch's health, soundness, temperament, and freedom from serious faults. A copy of her pedigree may be requested, as might a picture of her. A discussion of her background over the telephone may be sufficient to assure the stud's owner that she is suitable for the stud dog and of type, breeding, and quality herself to produce puppies of the quality for which the dog is noted. The owner of a top-quality stud is

Ch. Solitude Creek How About That, by Ch. Lyn-Mar Acres Press Agent ex Solitude Creek Crown Treasure, was born in August 1963. Won her championship with all major points, and was the dam of three champions all in one litter. Breeder-owner Alice B. Lane, Solitude Creek Kennels, Reston, Md.

often extremely selective in the bitches permitted to be bred to his dog, in an effort to keep the standard of his puppies high. The owner of a stud dog may require that the bitch be tested for brucellosis, which should be attended to not more than a month previous to the breeding.

Check out which airport will be most convenient for the person meeting and returning the bitch if she is to be shipped and also what airlines use that airport. You will find that the airlines are also apt to have special requirements concerning acceptance of animals for shipping. These include weather limitations and types of crates which are acceptable. The weather limits have to do with extreme heat and extreme cold at the point of destination, as some airlines will not fly dogs into temperatures above or below certain levels, fearing for their safety. The crate problem is a simple one, since if your own crate is not suitable, most of the airlines have specially designed crates available for purchase at a fair and moderate price. It is a good plan to purchase one of these if you intend to be shipping dogs with any sort of frequency. They are made of fiberglas and are the safest type to use for shipping.

Normally you must notify the airline several days in advance to make a reservation, as they are able to accommodate only a certain number of dogs on each flight. Plan on shipping the bitch on about her eighth or ninth day of season, but be careful to avoid shipping her on a weekend, when schedules often vary and freight offices are apt to be closed. Whenever you can, ship your bitch on a direct flight. Changing planes always carries a certain amount of risk of a dog being overlooked or wrongly routed at the middle stop, so avoid this danger if at all possible. The bitch must be accompanied by a health certificate which you must obtain from your veterinarian before taking her to the airport. Usually it will be necessary to have the bitch at the airport about two hours prior to flight time. Before finalizing arrangements, find out from the stud's owner at what time of day it will be most convenient to have the bitch picked up promptly upon arrival.

It is simpler if you can plan to bring the bitch to the stud dog. Some people feel that the trauma of the flight may cause the bitch to not conceive; and, of course, undeniably there is a slight risk in shipping which can be avoided if you are able to drive the bitch to her destination. Be sure to leave yourself sufficient time to assure your arrival at the right time for her for breeding (normally the tenth to fourteenth day following the first signs of color); and remember that if you want the bitch bred twice, you should allow a day to elapse between the two matings. Do not expect the stud's owner to house you while you are there. Locate a nearby motel that takes dogs and make that your headquarters.

Just prior to the time your bitch is due in season, you should take her to visit your veterinarian. She should be checked for worms and should receive all the booster shots for which she is due plus one for parvovirus, unless she has had the latter shot fairly recently. The brucellosis test can also be done then, and the health certificate can be obtained for shipping if she is to travel by air. Should the bitch be at all overweight, now is the time to get the surplus off. She should be in good condition, neither underweight nor overweight, at the time of breeding.

The moment you notice the swelling of the vulva, for which you should be checking daily as the time for her season approaches, and

272

Ch. Nasa's Shadrack of MiBerSham, C.D., owned by Bert & Mike Salyers and Diane Funk. This outstanding Basset was a strong contender in the Hound Group of the mid-seventies, winning many Groups and Bests in Show. He is shown winning his first Best in Show under judge Dennis Grivas. He was always handled by Jack H. Potts.

Ch. Bassett's Baggatelle in 1958, by Ch. Rossingham Barrister ex Bassett's Lady Schnoozer, the dam of three champions. Richard and Evelyn Bassett, Bothell, Washington.

the appearance of color, immediately contact the stud's owner and settle on the day for shipping or make the appointment for your arrival with the bitch for breeding. If you are shipping the bitch, the stud fee check should be mailed immediately, leaving ample time for it to have been received when the bitch arrives and the mating takes place. Be sure to call the airline making her reservation at that time, too.

Do not feed the bitch within a few hours before shipping her. Be certain that she has had a drink of water and been well exercised before closing her in the crate. Several layers of newspapers, topped with some shredded newspaper, make a good bed and can be discarded

274

when she arrives at her destination; these can be replaced with fresh newspapers for her return home. Remember that the bitch should be brought to the airport about two hours before flight time as sometimes the airlines refuse to accept late arrivals.

If you are taking your bitch by car, be certain that you will arrive at a reasonable time of day. Do not appear late in the evening. If your arrival in town is not until late, get a good night's sleep at your motel and contact the stud's owner first thing in the morning. If possible, leave children and relatives at home, as they will only be in the way and perhaps unwelcome by the stud's owner. Most stud dog owners prefer not to have any unnecessary people on hand during the actual mating.

Ch. Orange Park Roy winning a Hound Group in 1969 handled by Jerry Rigden for Oranpark Kennels, the Meyers, Orange, California.

Ch. Abbot Run Valley Pamela, by Ch. Intoxication of Blue Hill ex Abbot Run Valley Gabby, winning Best of Opposite Sex at the Potomac Basset Hound Club Specialty in 1967 handled by Barbara Wicklund, co-owner with Marjorie M. Brandt. This was Bar-Wick Kennels' foundation bitch. She was bred by Doris Hurry.

A mother-daughter team, Ch. Le Clair Merry Madelyn, U.D. and Ch. Bugle Bay's Souffle, U.D. owned by Bugle Bay Bassets, Jim and Margery Cook. Madelyn was the third Basset to attain her championship and U.D. Souffle was the fourth. There have been a total of only five Bassets to attain these titles as we write. Madelyn is by Ch. Barbara's J.P. Morgan Le Clair ex Hartshead Magnolia.

Ch. Galway Teresa, by Ch. Ebenezer of Hampden Meadows ex Galway Silhouette of Abbie, bred by Elizabeth K. Dexter, owned by Peter C.J. Martin, Libertyville, Illinois. Top Winning Basset Bitch for two years during her show career.

After the breeding has taken place, if you wish to sit and visit for awhile and the stud's owner has the time, return the bitch to her crate in your car (first ascertaining, of course, that the temperature is comfortable for her and that there is proper ventilation). She should not be permitted to urinate for at least one hour following the breeding. This is the time when you get the business part of the transaction attended to. Pay the stud fee, upon which you should receive your breeding certificate and, if you do not already have it, a copy of the stud dog's pedigree. The owner of the stud dog does not sign or furnish a litter registration application until the puppies have been born.

Upon your return home, you can settle down and plan in happy anticipation a wonderful litter of puppies. A word of caution! Remember that although she has been bred, your bitch is still an interesting target for all male dogs, so guard her carefully for the next week or until you are absolutely certain that her season has entirely ended. This would be no time to have any unfortunate incident with another dog.

The Basset Stud Dog

Choosing the best stud dog to complement your bitch is often very difficult. The two principal factors to be considered should be the stud's conformation and his pedigree. Conformation is fairly obvious; you want a dog that is typical of the breed in the words of the standard of perfection. Understanding pedigrees is a bit more subtle since the pedigree lists the ancestry of the dog and involves individuals and bloodlines with which you may not be entirely familiar.

To a novice in the breed, then, the correct interpretation of a pedigree may at first be difficult to grasp. Study the pictures and text of this book and you will find many names of important bloodlines and members of the breed. Also make an effort to discuss the various dogs behind the proposed stud with some of the more experienced breeders, starting with the breeder of your own bitch. Frequently these folks will be personally familiar with many of the dogs in question, can offer opinions of them, and may have access to additional pictures which you would benefit by seeing.

It is very important that the stud's pedigree should be harmonious with that of the bitch you plan on breeding to him. Do not rush out and breed to the latest winner with no thought of whether or not he can produce true quality. By no means are all great show dogs great producers. It is the producing record of the dog in question and the dogs and bitches from which he has come which should be the basis on which you make your choice.

Breeding dogs is never a money-making operation. By the time you pay a stud fee, care for the bitch during pregnancy, whelp the litter, and rear the puppies through their early shots, worming, and so on, you will be fortunate to break even financially once the puppies have been sold. Your chances of doing this are greater if you are breeding for a show-quality litter which will bring you higher prices as the pups are sold as show prospects. Therefore, your wisest investment is to use the best dog available for your bitch regardless of the cost; then you should wind up with more valuable puppies. Remember that it is equally costly to raise mediocre puppies as top ones, and your chances of financial return are better on the latter. To breed to the most excellent, most suitable stud dog you can find is the only sensible thing to do, and it is poor economy to quibble over the amount you are paying in stud fee.

It will be your decision which course you decide to follow when you breed your bitch, as there are three options: line-breeding, inbreeding,

Strathalbyn Hathaway, America's No. 2 Basset sire for 1982 with one litter all of which finished and won a Group or Group placement from the classes. Owned by Mr. and Mrs. Eric F. George, Crescent, Missouri.

Am. and Can. Ch. Siefenjagenheim Lazy Bones, by Ch. Lyn-Mar's Clown ex Webb's Black Amanda, owned by Chris G. Teeter and W. Frank Hardy, a triple Group Top Tenner sired 51 champions!

Ch. Strathalbyn Shoot To Kill, C.D., T.D. winning Best in Show at Taconia Hills in 1979, judge Mrs. Curtis Brown, handled by Joy S. Brewster. Owned by Strathalbyn Kennels, Mr. and Mrs. Eric George. "Michael" was No. 1 Basset Hound 1979, and became the first pack hound to win an all-breed Best in Show and the only No. 1 Basset to ever win titles in other disciplines. Michael has been Grand Champion Basset at the Bryn Mawr Hound Show, Highest Combined Score Field Performance, Bench Merit National Pack Trials, and undefeated in Brace Competition with his litter brother, Ch. Strathalbyn Coldstream Eric, who was also Grand Champion Basset at the Bryn Mawr Hound Show.

and outcrossing. Each of these methods has its supporters and its detractors! Line-breeding is breeding a bitch to a dog belonging originally to the same canine family, being descended from the same ancestors, such as half-brother to half-sister, grandsire to grand-daughters, niece to uncle (and vice-versa) or cousin to cousin. In-breeding is breeding father to daughter, mother to son, or full brother to sister. Outcross breeding is breeding a dog and a bitch with no or only a few mutual ancestors.

Line-breeding is probably the safest course, and the one most likely to bring results, for the novice breeder. The more sophisticated in-breeding should be left to the experienced, long-time breeders who thoroughly know and understand the risks and the possibilities in-volved with a particular line. It is usually done in an effort to intensify some ideal feature in that strain. Outcrossing is the reverse of in-breeding, an effort to introduce improvement in a specific feature needing correction, such as a shorter back, better movement, more correct head or coat, and so on.

It is the serious breeders' ambition to develop a strain or bloodline of their own, one strong in qualities for which their dogs will become distinguished. However, it must be realized that this will involve time, patience, and at least several generations before the achievement can be claimed. The safest way to embark on this plan, as we have men-tioned, is by the selection and breeding of one or two bitches, the best you can buy and from top-producing kennels. In the beginning you do *not* really have to own a stud dog. In the long run it is less expensive and sounder judgment to pay a stud fee when you are ready to breed a bitch than to purchase a stud dog and feed him all year; a stud dog does not win any popularity contests with owners of bitches to be bred until he becomes a champion, has been successfully Specialed for awhile, and has been at least moderately advertised, all of which adds up to a quite healthy expenditure.

The wisest course for the inexperienced breeder just starting out in dogs is as we have outlined above. Keep the best bitch puppy from the first several litters. After that you may wish to consider keeping your own stud dog if there has been a particularly handsome male in one of your litters that you feel has great potential or if you know where there is one available that you are interested in, with the feeling that he would work in nicely with the breeding program on which you have embarked. By this time, with several litters already born, your eye should have developed to a point enabling you to make a wise choice, either from one of your own litters or from among dogs you have seen that appear suitable.

The greatest care should be taken in the selection of your own stud dog. He must be of true type and highest quality as he may be responsible for siring many puppies each year, and he should come from a line of excellent dogs on both sides of his pedigree which themselves are, and which are descended from, successful producers. This dog should have no glaring faults in conformation; he should be of such quality that he can hold his own in keenest competition within his proven sire able to transmit his correct qualities to his puppies. Need we say that such a dog will be enormously expensive unless you have the good fortune to produce him in one of your own litters? To buy and use a lesser stud dog, however, is downgrading your breeding program unnecessarily since there are so many dogs fitting the description of a fine stud whose services can be used on payment of a stud fee. fine stud whose services can be used on payment of a stud fee.

You should *never* breed to an unsound dog or one with any serious standard or disqualifying faults. Not all champions by any means pass along their best features; and by the same token, occasionally you will find a great one who can pass along his best features but never gained his championship title due to some unusual circumstances. The information you need about a stud dog is what type of puppies he has produced and with what bloodlines and whether or not he possesses the bloodlines and attributes considered characteristic of the best in your breed.

If you go out to buy a stud dog, obviously he will not be a puppy but rather a fully mature and proven male with as many of the best attributes as possible. True, he will be an expensive investment, but if you choose and make his selection with care and forethought, he may well prove to be one of the best investments you have ever made.

Of course, the most exciting of all is when a young male you have decided to keep from one of your litters due to his tremendous show potential turns out to be a stud dog such as we have described. In this case he should be managed with care, for he is a valuable property that can contribute inestimably to his breed as a whole and to your own kennel specifically.

Do not permit your stud dog to be used until he is about a year old, and even then he should be bred to a mature, proven matron accustomed to breeding who will make his first experience pleasant and easy. A young dog can be put off forever by a maiden bitch who fights and resists his advances. Never allow this to happen. Always start a

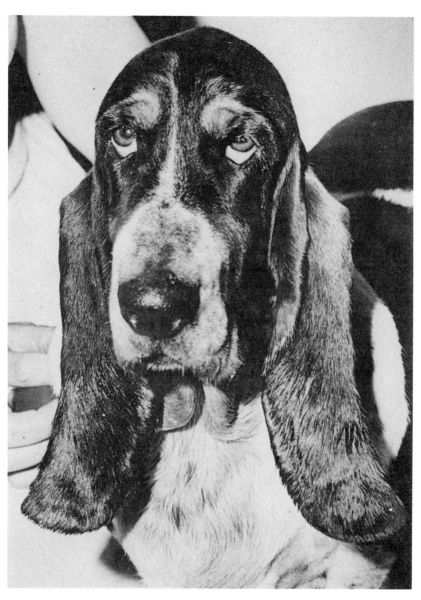

Ch. Lyn Mar Acres Bat Wing in 1971. Breeder-owner, Mrs. Margaret S. Walton, Mt. Holly, New Jersey.

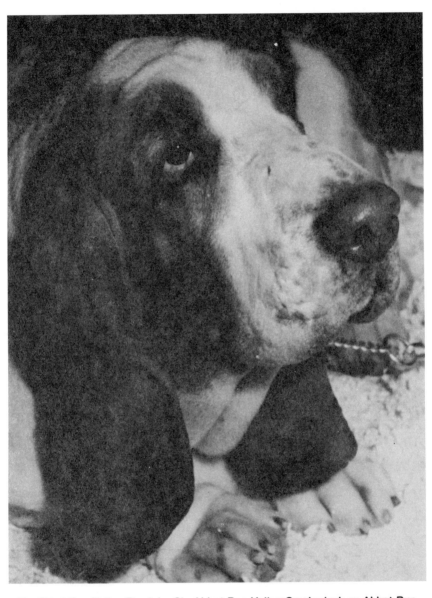

Ch. Abbot Run Valley Pearl, by Ch. Abbot Run Valley Crackerjack ex Abbot Run Valley Anita, owned by William L. Barton, Holmdel, New Jersey.

Lyn Mar Acres Dauntless at seven months of age, the afternoon he left for England where he was imported by the Basset Hound Club of England from his breeder Mrs. Margaret S. Walton, Mt. Holly, New Jersey.

stud dog out with a bitch who is mature, has been bred previously, and is of even temperament. The first breeding should be performed in quiet surroundings with only you and one other person to hold the bitch. Do not make it a circus, as the experience will determine the dog's outlook about future stud work. If he does not enjoy the first experience or associates it with any unpleasantness, you may well have a problem in the future.

Your young stud must permit help with the breeding, as later there will be bitches who will not be cooperative. If right from the beginning you are there helping him and praising him whether or not your assistance is actually needed, he will expect and accept this as a matter of course when a difficult bitch comes along.

Ch. Forestbay Orvil of Manor Hill, ROM, bred by Joan C. and Ronald H. Scholz. Owned by Forestbay Kennels. By Ch. Abbot Run Valley Brassy ex Ch. Bonnie Ridge Fire-Bird. A Top Producer in the U.S. and Canada. Dorothy Hardy handling. Chris Teeter the judge at the Long Island Basset Hound Club Specialty in 1967.

Things to have handy before introducing your dog and the bitch are K-Y jelly (the only lubricant which should be used) and a length of gauze with which to muzzle the bitch should it be necessary to keep her from biting you or the dog. Some bitches put up a fight; others are calm. It is best to be prepared.

At the time of the breeding the stud fee comes due, and it is expected that it will be paid promptly. Normally a return service is offered in case the bitch misses or fails to produce one live puppy. Conditions of the service are what the stud dog's owner makes them, and there are no standard rules covering this. The stud fee is paid for the act, not the result. If the bitch fails to conceive, it is customary for the owner to offer a free return service; but this is a courtesy and not to be considered a right, particularly in the case of a proven stud who is siring consistently and whose fault the failure obviously is *not*. Stud dog owners are always anxious to see their clients get good value and to have in the ring winning young stock by their dog; therefore, very few refuse to mate the second time. It is wise, however, for both parties to have the terms of the transaction clearly understood at the time of the breeding.

If the return service has been provided and the bitch has missed a second time, that is considered to be the end of the matter and the owner would be expected to pay a further fee if it is felt that the bitch should be given a third chance with the stud dog. The management of a stud dog and his visiting bitches is quite a task, and a stud fee has usually been well earned when one service has been achieved, let alone by repeated visits from the same bitch.

The accepted litter is one live puppy. It is wise to have printed a breeding certificate which the owner of the stud dog and the owner of the bitch both sign. This should list in detail the conditions of the breeding as well as the dates of the mating.

Upon occasion, arrangements other than a stud fee in cash are made for a breeding, such as the owner of the stud taking a pick-of-the-litter puppy in lieu of money. This should be clearly specified on the breeding certificate along with the terms of the age at which the stud's owner will select the puppy, whether it is to be a specific sex, or whether it is to be the pick of the entire litter.

The price of a stud fee varies according to circumstances. Usually, to prove a young stud dog, his owner will allow the first breeding to be quite inexpensive. Then, once a bitch has become pregnant by him, he becomes a "proven stud" and the fee rises accordingly for bitches that follow. The sire of championship-quality puppies will bring a stud fee of at least the purchase price of one show puppy as the accepted "rule-of-thumb." Until at least one champion by your stud dog has finished, the fee will remain equal to the price of one pet puppy. When his list of champions starts to grow, so does the amount of the stud fee. For a top-producing sire of champions, the stud fee will rise accordingly.

Almost invariably it is the bitch who comes to the stud dog for the breeding. Immediately upon having selected the stud dog you wish to use, discuss the possibility with the owner of that dog. It is the stud dog owner's prerogative to refuse to breed any bitch deemed unsuitable for his dog. Stud fee and method of payment should be stated at this time, and a decision reached on whether it is to be a full cash transaction at the time of the mating or a pick-of-the-litter puppy, usually at eight weeks of age.

If the owner of the stud dog must travel to an airport to meet the bitch and ship her for the flight home, an additional charge will be made for time, tolls, and gasoline based on the stud owner's proximity to the airport. The stud fee includes board for the day on the bitch's arrival through two days for breeding, with a day in between. If it is necessary that the bitch remain longer, it is very likely that additional board will be charged at the normal per-day rate for the breed.

Be sure to advise the stud's owner as soon as you know that your bitch is in season so that the stud dog will be available. This is especially important because if he is a dog being shown, he and his owner may be unavailable owing to the dog's absence from home.

As the owner of a stud dog being offered to the public, it is essential that you have proper facilities for the care of visiting bitches. Nothing can be worse than a bitch being insecurely housed and slipping out to become lost or bred by the wrong dog. If you are taking people's valued bitches into your kennel or home, it is imperative that you provide them with comfortable, secure housing and good care while they are your responsibility.

There is no dog more valuable than the proven sire of champions, Group winners, and Best in Show dogs. Once you have such an animal, guard his reputation well and do *not* permit him to be bred to just any bitch that comes along. It takes two to make the puppies; even the most dominant stud can not do it all himself, so never permit him to breed a bitch you consider unworthy. Remember that when the puppies arrive, it will be your stud dog who will be blamed for any lack of quality, while the bitch's shortcomings will be quickly and conveniently overlooked.

Ch. Windmaker's Summer Storm, who combines Lyn Mar Acres, Santana-Mandeville, Hubertus and Lime Tree breeding is one of the excellent Bassets owned by James R. and Wanda A. White.

Ch. Beaujangle's Chance, by Am. and Can. Ch. Supai's Sleeping Rainbow ex Ch. Luxembourg's Cassandra, one of the current studs at Beaujangle. Owners, Diane Malenfant and Claudia Lane, Glendale, Arizona.

Going into the actual management of the mating is a bit superfluous here. If you have had previous experience in breeding a dog and bitch you will know how the mating is done. If you do not have such experience, you should not attempt to follow directions given in a book but should have a veterinarian, breeder friend, or handler there to help you the first few times. You do not just turn the dog and bitch loose together and await developments, as too many things can go wrong and you may altogether miss getting the bitch bred. Someone should hold the dog and the bitch (one person each) until the "tie" is made and these two people should stay with them during the entire act.

If you get a complete tie, probably only the one mating is absolutely necessary. However, especially with a maiden bitch or one that has come a long distance for this breeding, we prefer following up with a second breeding, leaving one day in between the two matings. In this way there will be little or no chance of the bitch missing.

Once the tie has been completed and the dogs release, be certain that the male's penis goes completely back within its sheath. He should be allowed a drink of water and a short walk, and then he should be put into his crate or somewhere alone where he can settle down. Do not allow him to be with other dogs for a while as they will notice the odor of the bitch on him, and particularly with other males present, he may become involved in a fight.

Pregnancy, Whelping, and the Litter

Once the bitch has been bred and is back at home, remember to keep an ever watchful eye that no other male gets to her until at least the twenty-second day of her season has passed. Until then, it will still be possible for an unwanted breeding to take place, which at this point would be catastrophic. Remember that she actually can have two separate litters by two different dogs, so take care.

In other ways, she should be treated normally. Controlled exercise is good, and necessary for the bitch throughout her pregnancy, tapering it off to just several short walks daily, preferably on lead, as she reaches about her seventh week. As her time grows close, be careful about her jumping or playing too roughly.

The theory that a bitch should be overstuffed with food when pregnant is a poor one. A fat bitch is never an easy whelper, so the overfeeding you consider good for her may well turn out to be the exact opposite. During the first few weeks of pregnancy, your bitch should be fed her normal diet. At four to five weeks along, calcium

Ch. Wagtails Rise and Shine placing second in the Hound Group at Durham in 1983. Handled by Joy S. Brewster for owners Mr. and Mrs. Alfred A. Wicklund and Mary Louise Chipman. By Ch. Bar-Wick's First Baseman ex Champion Wagtail's Mischief Maker. Born 1980, bred by the Chipmans.

Ch. Stoneybluff Monarch taking a Group 3rd in 1981. This splendid dog completed his title at the Fort Dearborn Specialty under breeder-judge Joe Braun. Breeder-owners, Frank and Virginia Kovalic.

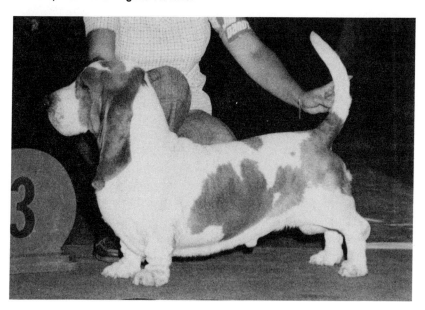

The great Ch. Tal-E-Ho's Top Banana, by Ch. Tal-E-Ho's Prancer ex Tal-E-Ho's Dorinda, bred by Henry Jerman and Mark Dembrow, owned by Peter C.J. Martin and Bryan K. Martin. A Best in Show winner; 13 times Best in Specialty Show; 15 times First in Hound Group; 76 Group placements; and 152 times Best of Breed.

Am. and Can. Ch. Solitude Creek Sophocles, by Ch. Lyn-Mar Acres M'Lord Batuff ex Ch. Solitude Creek How Bout That, born July 1967, bred and owned by Alice B. Lane, Reston, Maryland.

should be added to her food. At seven weeks her food may be increased if she seems to crave more than she is getting, and a meal of canned milk (mixed with an equal amount of water) should be introduced. If she is fed just once a day, add another meal rather than overload her with too much at one time. If twice a day is her schedule, then a bit more food can be added to each feeding.

A week before the pups are due, your bitch should be introduced to her whelping box so that she will be accustomed to it and feel at home there when the puppies arrive. She should be encouraged to sleep there but permitted to come and go as she wishes. The box should be roomy enough for her to lie down and stretch out but not too large lest the pups have more room than is needed in which to roam and possibly get chilled by going too far away from their mother. Be sure that the box has a "pig rail"; this will prevent the puppies from being crushed against the sides. The room in which the box is placed, either in your home or in the kennel, should be kept at about 70 degrees Fahrenheit. In winter it may be necessary to have an infrared lamp over the whelping box, in which case be careful not to place it too low or close to the puppies.

Newspapers will become a very important commodity, so start collecting them well in advance to have a big pile handy to the whelping box. With a litter of puppies, one never seems to have papers enough, so the higher pile to start with, the better off you will be. Other necessities for whelping time are clean, soft turkish towels, scissors, and a bottle of alcohol.

You will know that her time is very near when your bitch becomes restless, wandering in and out of her box and of the room. She may refuse food, and at that point her temperature will start to drop. She will dig at and tear up the newspapers in her box, shiver, and generally look uncomfortable. Only you should be with your bitch at this time. She does not need spectators; and several people, even though they may be family members whom she knows, hanging over her may upset her to the point where she may harm the puppies. You should remain nearby, quietly watching, not fussing or hovering; speak calmly and frequently to her to instill confidence. Eventually she will settle down in her box and begin panting; contractions will follow. Soon thereafter a puppy will start to emerge, sliding out with the contractions. The mother immediately should open the sac, sever the cord with her teeth, and then clean up the puppy. She will also eat the placenta, which you should permit. Once the puppy is cleaned, it should be placed next to the bitch unless she is showing signs of having the next one immediately. Almost at once the puppy will start looking for a nipple on which to nurse, and you should ascertain that it is able to latch on successfully.

If the puppy is a breech (*i.e.,* born feet first), you must watch carefully for it to be completely delivered as quickly as possible and the sac removed quickly so that the puppy does not drown. Sometimes even a normally positioned birth will seem extremely slow in coming. Should this occur, you might take a clean towel and, as the bitch contracts, pull the puppy out, doing so gently and with utmost care. If, once the puppy is delivered, it shows little signs of life, take a rough turkish towel and massage the puppy's chest by rubbing quite briskly back and forth. Continue this for about fifteen minutes, and be sure that the mouth is free from liquid. It may be necessary to try mouth-to-mouth breathing, which is done by pressing the puppy's jaws open and, using a finger, depressing the tongue which may be stuck to the roof of the mouth. Then place your mouth against the puppy's and blow hard down the puppy's throat. Bubbles may pop out of its nose, but keep on blowing. Rub the puppy's chest with the towel again and try artificial respiration, pressing the sides of the chest together slowly and rhythmically—in and out, in and out. Keep trying one method or the other for at least twenty minutes before giving up. You may be rewarded with a live puppy who otherwise would not have made it.

If you are successful in bringing the puppy around, do not immediately put it back with the mother as it should be kept extra warm. Put it in a cardboard box on an electric heating pad or, if it is the time of year when your heat is running, near a radiator or near the fireplace or stove. As soon as the rest of the litter has been born it then can join the others.

An hour or more may elapse between puppies, which is fine so long as the bitch seems comfortable and is neither straining nor contracting. She should not be permitted to remain unassisted for more than an hour if she does continue to contract. This is when you should get her to your veterinarian, whom you should already have alerted to the possibility of a problem existing. He should examine her and perhaps give her a shot of Pituitrin. In some cases the veterinarian may find that a Caesarean section is necessary due to a puppy being lodged in a manner making normal delivery impossible. Sometimes this is caused by an abnormally large puppy, or it may just be that the puppy is simply turned in the wrong position. If the bitch does require a

Ch. Orange Park Dexter, by Ch. Santana-Mandeville's Tarzan ex Hartshead May-belline, a very famous winner of the late 1960's owned by Oranpark Bassets, Orange, California. Photo courtesy of Mrs. Meyer.

One of Patricia Fellman's Basset favorites, Courtside Francaise, C.D., needed but one major to finish when Pat gave her to a friend and never did get this lovely bitch out to the shows again. A pity, as she was one of much quality.

Ch. Lyn Mar Acres Sir Michelob and Ch. Lyn Mar Acres April Showers at play in the kennel yard. Both homebreds owned by Margaret S. Walton, Mt. Holly, New Jersey.

296

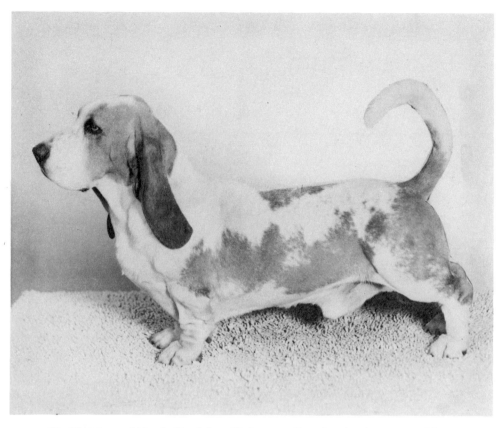

Ch. Gladstone of Mandeville. A beautifully proportioned male who was used in a "Visualization of the Standards" in the 1960's. Owned by Mr. and Mrs. Paul Nelson, Santana-Mandeville Kennels. Photo courtesy of Dr. and Mrs. Leonard Skolnick.

Caesarean section, the puppies already born must be kept warm in their cardboard box with a heating pad under the box.

Once the section is done, get the bitch and the puppies home. Do not attempt to put the puppies in with the bitch until she has regained consciousness as she may unknowingly hurt them. But do get them back to her as soon as possible for them to start nursing.

Should the mother lack milk at this time, the puppies must be fed by hand, kept very warm, and held onto the mother's teats several times a day in order to stimulate and encourage the secretion of milk, which should start shortly.

Ch. Mattie's Quercus, C.D., in 1957 enjoying the life of retirement. Owned by Richard and Evelyn Bassett.

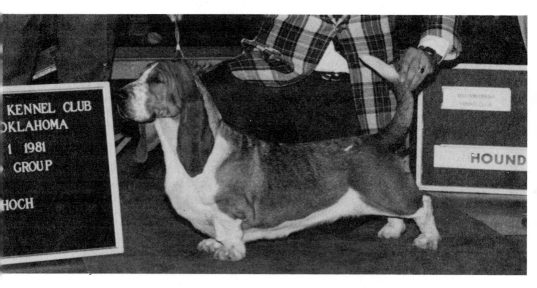

Ch. Denmar's Snickers, by Ch. Rodi's Sir Reggie of Mammoth ex Ch. Hooper-Knoll's Dinah Mite. Bred by Dennis and Marie Krondack; owned by Peter C.J. Martin, Bryan K. Martin, and Sherry Neiberger. 1980 National Sweepstakes winner.

Ch. Lyn Mar Acres Top Brass, Best of Breed. Ch. Pride of Lyn Mar Acres Best of Opposite Sex. An exciting double victory for Mrs. Margaret S. Walton, Mt. Holly, N.J. at Westminster in 1955.

Field Ch. Bugle Bay's Much Ado, C.D., T.D., taking High in Trial at the Basset Hound Club of America in 1981. Francis and Ruth Paule, owners, Riverton, Illinois.

Assuming that there has been no problem and that the bitch has whelped naturally, you should insist that she go out to exercise, staying just long enough to make herself comfortable. She can be offered a bowl of milk and a biscuit, but then she should settle down with her family. Freshen the whelping box for her with fresh newspapers while she is taking this respite so that she and the puppies will have a clean bed.

Unless some problem arises, there is little you must do about the puppies until they become three to four weeks old. Keep the box clean and supplied with fresh newspapers the first few days, but then turkish towels should be tacked down to the bottom of the box so that the puppies will have traction as they move about.

If the bitch has difficulties with her milk supply, or if you should be so unfortunate as to lose her, then you must be prepared to either hand-feed or tube-feed the puppies if they are to survive. We personally prefer tube-feeding as it is so much faster and easier. If the bitch is available, it is best that she continues to clean and care for the puppies in the normal manner excepting for the food supplements you will provide. If it is impossible for her to do this, then after every feeding you must gently rub each puppy's abdomen with wet cotton to make it urinate, and the rectum should be gently rubbed to open the bowels.

Newborn puppies must be fed every three to four hours around the clock. The puppies must be kept warm during this time. Have your veterinarian teach you how to tube-feed. You will find that it is really quite simple.

After a normal whelping, the bitch will require additional food to enable her to produce sufficient milk. In addition to being fed twice daily, she should be given some canned milk several times each day.

When the puppies are two weeks old, their nails should be clipped, as they are needle sharp at this age and can hurt or damage the mother's teats and stomach as the pups hold on to nurse.

Between three and four weeks of age, the puppies should begin to be weaned. Scraped beef (prepared by scraping it off slices of beef with a spoon so that none of the gristle is included) may be offered in very small quantities a couple of times daily for the first few days. Then by the third day you can mix puppy chow with warm water as directed on the package, offering it four times daily. By now the mother should be kept away from the puppies and out of the box for several hours at a time so that when they have reached five weeks of age she is left in with them only overnight. By the time the puppies are six weeks old, they should be entirely weaned and receiving only occasional visits from their mother.

Most veterinarians recommend a temporary DHL (distemper, hepatitis, leptospirosis) shot when the puppies are six weeks of age. This remains effective for about two weeks. Then at eight weeks of age, the puppies should receive the series of permanent shots for DHL protection. It is also a good idea to discuss with your vet the advisability of having your puppies inoculated against the dreaded parvovirus at the same time. Each time the pups go to the vet for shots, you should bring stool samples so that they can be examined for worms. Worms go through various stages of development and may be present in a stool sample even though the sample does not test positive in every checkup. So do not neglect to keep careful watch on this.

The puppies should be fed four times daily until they are three months old. Then you can cut back to three feedings daily. By the time the puppies are six months of age, two meals daily are sufficient. Some people feed their dogs twice daily throughout their lifetime; others go to one meal daily when the puppy becomes one year of age.

The ideal age for puppies to go to their new homes is between eight and twelve weeks, although some puppies successfully adjust to a new home when they are six weeks old. Be sure that they go to their new owners accompanied by a description of the diet you've been feeding them and a schedule of the shots they have already received and those they still need. These should be included with the registration application and a copy of the pedigree.

Dr. Byron Wisner with Ch. Beartooth Victor.

Chapter 16

Traveling with Your Basset

When you travel with your dog, to shows or on vacation or wherever, remember that everyone does not share our enthusiasm or love for dogs and that those who do not, strange creatures though they seem to us, have their rights, too. These rights, on which we should not encroach, include not being disturbed, annoyed, or made uncomfortable by the presence and behavior of other people's pets. Your dog should be kept on lead in public places and should recognize and promptly obey the commands "Down," "Come," "Sit," and "Stay."

Take along his crate if you are going any distance with your dog. And keep him in it when riding in the car. A crated dog has a far better chance of escaping injury than one riding loose in the car should an accident occur or an emergency arise. If you do permit your dog to ride loose, never allow him to hang out a window, ears blowing in the breeze. An injury to his eyes could occur in this manner. He could also become overly excited by something he sees and jump out, or he could lose his balance and fall out.

Never, ever under any circumstances, should a dog be permitted to ride loose in the back of a pick-up truck. It is horrible that some people do transport dogs in this manner which is cruel and shocking. How easily such a dog can be thrown out of the truck by sudden jolts or an impact! And that many dogs have jumped out at the sight of something exciting along the way is certain. Some unthinking individuals tie the dog, probably not realizing that were he to jump under those circumstances, his neck would be broken, he could be dragged alongside the vehicle, or he could be hit by another vehicle. If you are for any

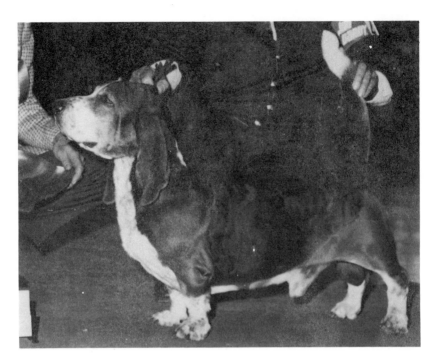

Ch. Bret Mavrik of Rockin Pas, T.D. winning the Veteran's Class at the South Florida Basset Hound Specialty in 1976. Owned by Mr. and Mrs. Billy Wray, Jupiter, Florida.

Ch. Manor Hill Top Spot, ROM, lived only four and a half years, but long enough to become a pillar of the breed, producing two National Specialty winners (Ch. Kazoo Galloping Gitch and Ch. Manor Hill Fringe Benefit). By Ch. Abbot Run Valley Brassy ex Ch. Bonnie Ridge Fire-Bird. Bred and owned by Joan C. and Ronald H. Scholz, Manor Hill Bassets, Stratford, Conneticut.

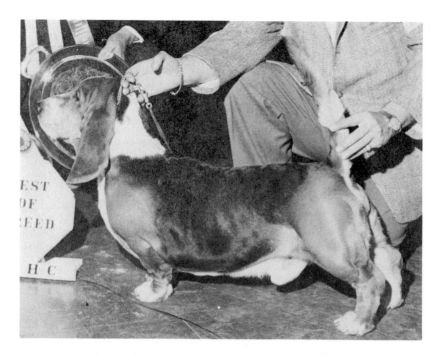

The great Ch. The Ring's Ali Baba on one of his numerous wins. This noted Basset is owned by Mrs. Frances Scaife and handled by Jerry Rigden.

Ch. Santana-Mandeville Rodney, winning Best Hound at Harford County in April 1965. A son of those famed producers Ch. Santana-Mandeville Tarzan and Ch. Gwendolyn of Mandeville, Rodney was the leading Basset winner in Group competition for that period.

These are all obedience winners from the kennels of Jim and Margery Cook at Azle, Texas. *Left to right,* Bugle Bay's Casserole (a Souffle daughter); Ch. Le Claire's Merry Madelyn, U.D., the Cook's first champion; Ch. Bugle Bay's Bouillon, C.D.X., T.D., ROM, also with field points, an Annie son; and Ch. Bugle Bay's Ado Annie, C.D., again with field points, a Madelyn daughter.

reason taking your dog in an open back truck, please have sufficient regard for that dog to at least provide a crate for him, and then remember that, in or out of a crate, a dog riding under the direct rays of the sun in hot weather can suffer and have his life endangered by the heat.

If you are staying at a hotel or motel with your dog, exercise him somewhere other than in the flower beds and parking lot of the property. People walking to and from their cars really are not thrilled at "stepping in something" left by your dog. Should an accident occur, pick it up with a tissue or a paper towel and deposit it in a proper receptacle; do not just walk off leaving it to remain there. Usually there are grassy areas on the sides of and behind motels where dogs can be exercised. Use them rather than the more conspicuous, usually carefully tended, front areas or those close to the rooms. If you are becoming a dog show enthusiast, you will eventually need an exercise pen to take with you to the show. Exercise pens are ideal to use when staying at motels, too, as they permit you to limit the dog's roaming space and to pick up after him more easily.

Never leave your dog unattended in the room of a motel unless you are absolutely, positively certain that he will stay there quietly and not damage or destroy anything. You do not want a long list of complaints from irate guests, caused by the annoying barking or whining of a lonesome dog in strange surroundings or an overzealous watch dog barking furiously each time a footstep passes the door or he hears a sound from an adjoining room. And you certainly do not want to return to torn curtains or bedspreads, soiled rugs, or other embarrassing evidence of the fact that your dog is not really house-reliable after all.

If yours is a dog accustomed to traveling with you and you are positive that his behavior will be acceptable when left alone, that is fine. But if the slightest uncertainty exists, the wise course is to leave him in the car while you go to dinner or elsewhere; then bring him into the room when you are ready to retire for the night.

When you travel with a dog, it is often simpler to take along from home the food and water he will need rather than buying food and looking for water while you travel. In this way he will have the rations to which he is accustomed and which you know agree with him, and there will be no fear of problems due to different drinking water. Feeding on the road is quite easy now, at least for short trips, with all the splendid dry prepared foods and high-quality canned meats available. A variety of lightweight, refillable water containers can be bought at many types of stores.

If you are going to another country, you will need a health certificate from your veterinarian for each dog you are taking with you, certifying that each has had rabies shots within the required time preceding your visit.

Be careful always to leave sufficient openings to ventilate your car when the dog will be alone in it. Remember that during the summer, the rays of the sun can make an inferno of a closed car within only a few minutes, so leave enough window space open to provide air circulation. Again, if your dog is in a crate, this can be done quite safely. The fact that you have left the car in a shady spot is not always a guarantee that you will find conditions the same when you return. Don't forget that the position of the sun changes in a matter of minutes, and the car you left nicely shaded half an hour ago can be getting full sunlight far more quickly than you may realize. So, if you leave a dog in the car, make sure there is sufficient ventilation and check back frequently to ascertain that all is well.

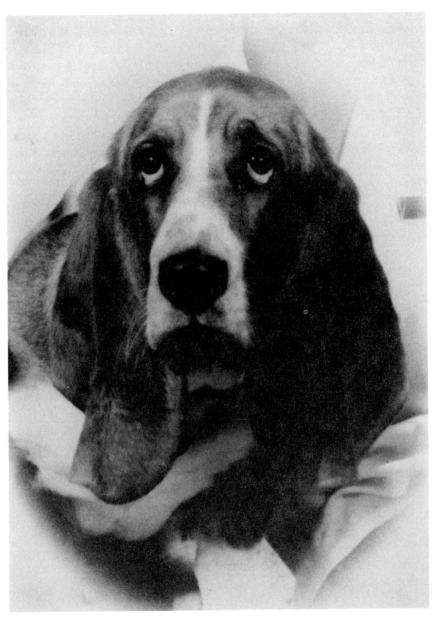

Headstudy of Joan Urban's first Basset, Mex. and Am. Ch. Monsieur Pierre La Rue, whelped in 1969 who lived to be fourteen years of age.

Chapter 17

Responsibilities of Breeders and Owners

The first responsibility of any person breeding dogs is to do so with care, forethought, and deliberation. It is inexcusable to breed more litters than you need to carry on your show program or to perpetuate your bloodlines. A responsible breeder should not cause a litter to be born without definite plans for the safe and happy disposition of the puppies.

A responsible dog breeder makes absolutely certain, so far as is humanly possible, that the home to which one of his puppies will go is a good home, one that offers proper care and an enthusiastic owner. We have tremendous admiration for those people who insist on visiting (although doing so is not always feasible) the prospective owners of their puppies, to see if they have suitable facilities for keeping a dog, that they understand the responsibility involved, and that all members of the household are in accord regarding the desirability of owning one. All breeders should carefully check out the credentials of prospective purchasers to be sure that the puppy is being placed in responsible hands.

We are certain that no breeder ever wants a puppy or grown dog he has raised to wind up in an animal shelter, in an experimental laboratory, or as a victim of a speeding car. While complete control of such a situation may be impossible, it is at least our responsibility to make every effort to turn over dogs to responsible people. When selling a puppy, it is a good idea to do so with the understanding that should it become necessary to place the dog in other hands, the purchaser will first contact you, the breeder. You may want to help in some way, possibly by buying or taking back the dog or placing it elsewhere. It is not fair just to sell our puppies and then never again give a thought to their welfare. Family problems arise, people may be forced to move where dogs are prohibited, or people just plain grow bored with a dog and its care. Thus the dog becomes a victim. You, as the dog's breeder, should concern yourself with the welfare of each of your dogs and see to it that the dog remains in good hands.

The final obligation every dog owner shares, be there just one dog or an entire kennel involved, is that of making detailed, explicit plans for the future of our dearly loved animals in the event of the owner's death. Far too many of us are apt to procrastinate and leave this very important matter unattended to, feeling that everything will work out or that "someone will see to them." The latter is not too likely, at least not to the benefit of the dogs, unless you have done some advance planning which will assure their future well-being.

Life is filled with the unexpected, and even the youngest, healthiest, most robust of us may be the victim of a fatal accident or sudden illness. The fate of our dogs, so entirely in our hands, should never be left to chance. If you have not already done so, please get together with your lawyer and set up a clause in your will specifying what you want done with each of your dogs, to whom they will be entrusted (after first making absolutely certain that the person selected is willing and able to assume the responsibility), and telling the locations of all registration papers, pedigrees, and kennel records. Just think of the possibilities which might happen otherwise! If there is another family member who shares your love of the dogs, that is good and you have less to worry about. But if your heirs are not dog-oriented, they will hardly know how to proceed or how to cope with the dogs themselves, and they may wind up disposing of or caring for your dogs in a manner that would break your heart were you around to know about it.

In our family, we have specific instructions in each of our wills for each of our dogs. A friend, also a dog person who regards her own dogs with the same concern and esteem as we do ours, has agreed to take over their care until they can be placed accordingly and will make certain that all will work out as we have planned. We have this person's name and phone number prominently displayed in our van and car and in our wallets. Our lawyer is aware of this fact. It is all spelled out in our wills. The friend has a signed check of ours to be used in case of an emergency or accident when we are traveling with the dogs; this check will be used to cover her expense to come and take

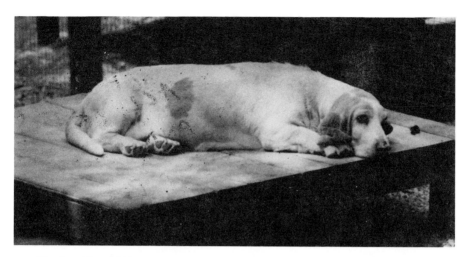

Tantivvy Blond Sidonia, age 12 years, by Ch. Lyn-Mar Acres Joker's Wild ex Tantivy Denise, is the dam of Ch. Strathalbyn Shoot To Kill, C.D., T.D. and Ch. Strathalbyn Cold Spring Eric. "Blondie" hunted the 1983-84 season three times a week. Owned by Mr. and Mrs. Eric F. George, Strathalbyn, Crescent, Missouri.

An informal shot of Ch. Santana-Mandeville's Rodney at the Alexandria Dog Show in 1965, courtesy of Dr. and Mrs. Leonard Skolnick.

This handsome dog was the second Basset to win Best in Show honors in the United States. Ch. Greenore's Joker, born in 1953, was by Margaret S. Walton's famed Ch. Lyn Mar's Clown from Success of Lyn Mar Acres. A Westminster Best of Breed winner, Joker was bred and owned by Mrs. Lee Hanlon, Westport, Conn., and handled by Johnny Davis.

Perfect relaxation on the couch! One of the Slippery Hill Bassets enjoying a nap. The Leonard Skolnicks, owners, Harwood, Maryland.

over the care of our dogs should anything happen to make it impossible for us to do so. This, we feel, is the least any dog owner should do in preparation for the time our dogs suddenly find themselves without us. There have been so many sad cases of dogs unprovided for by their loving owners, left to heirs who couldn't care less and who disposed of them in any way at all to get rid of them, or left to heirs who kept and neglected them under the misguided idea that they were providing them "a fine home with lots of freedom." All of us *must* prevent any of these misfortunes befalling our own dogs who have meant so much to us!

Index

Turner, Alan & Dorothy, 63

U

Upland (kennel), 28

Urban, Joan, 68, 69, 70, 150, 187, 238, 268, 308

V

Variety Group, 225

Veterans Class, 229

Veterinarian, 194, 272, 307

Vinson, Arthur & Susan, 108

W

Wade, Lee S., 28, 72

Walbridge, O. II, 32

Walhampton Pack, 14, 17

Walton, Mrs. Lynwood, 32, 55

Walton, Mrs. Margaret S., 68, 71, 72, 73, 94, 158, 283, 285, 296, 299, 312

Wardle, Arthur, 129

Washington, George, 26

Watson, Herbert, 16

Watson, Isabel & George, 58

Watts, Jean Williams, 51

Weaver, Linda & Peter, 122

Webb, Mrs. Lester Noel, 32

Weeks, Madison, 113

Wells, Ray D., Jr. & Louise, 47, 182

Westerby Pack, 17

Whelping, 293, 294

White, James R. & Wanda A., 110, 111, 112, 113, 153, 171, 221, 228, 289

Wicklund, Mr. & Mrs. Alfred, 36, 37, 159, 291

Wicklund, Barbara, 108, 276

Wickstrom, Mrs. Queenie, 237

Willer, Pat, 179

Willis, Dorothy, 108

Windmaker (kennel), 81, 110-113

Winner's Bitch, 222, 225

Winner's Class, 221

Winner's Dog, 22, 225

Wisner, Dr. Byron, 87, 199, 302

Wisner, Dr. Byron & Carol Sue, 39, 40, 41

Wolver (kennel), 99

Woodward, Jeanette, 179

Worms, 272

Wray, Lena, 246, 251

Wray, Lena & Billy, 248, 304

Wylie, Jean, 68